THE FORTUNE TELLER'S GUIDE TO SUCCESS

Creating A Wonderful Career As A Psychic

VALENTINA BURTON

The Fortune Teller of Dallas

Lucky Mojo Curio Company
Forestville, California

❖ 2018 ❖

The Fortune Teller's Guide to Success:
Creating A Wonderful Career As A Psychic
by Valentina Burton

© 2011, 2012, 2018 Valentina Burton
ValentinaBurton.com

Text: Valentina Burton, with catherine yronwode

Editor: catherine yronwode

Cover : Charles C. Dawson (art), Grey Townsend (book design)

Production: Valentina Burton, catherine yronwode, nagasiva yronwode

Illustrations: Various photographers

Code of Ethics and Code of Conduct on pages 83 - 84 reprinted by permission of the Association of Independent Readers and Rootworkers
ReadersAndRootworkers.org

First Printing 2011, Revised and Expanded Second Printing 2012
Third Printing 2017, Fourth Printing 2018, Fifth Printing 2021

Originally Published by Mystic Amusements Publishing, Dallas, Texas

Published by
The Lucky Mojo Curio Company
6632 Covey Road
Forestville, California 95436
LuckyMojo.com

ISBN: 978-0-9997809-1-6
Printed in Canada.

Dedication

This slim volume is dedicated to my best friend and business partner David Alexandre; my incredibly supportive parents (imagine having a daughter with not one oddball career, but two!), Tom for help with my insane idea to self-publish; nagasiva for book production; Niki, George, Tamara, Elizabeth, Ben, Vaughan, Judie, Suzy, Carolyn, Charlie, Katrina, Maven, Laura, Lauren, Rebecca, Tosh, Gina, Marin, Cheryl, Mistria, and the Gang at Hotel Zaza; my son (the irrepressible "Zerp" Rainone), and The World's Most Inspiring Teacher: cat yronwode.

I love you all more than words can express.

Table of Contents

Introduction

I never meant to write a book.

All of my intentions were always about becoming the very best card reader, palm reader, astrologer, and "divination specialist" possible.

Work never really feels like work when you love what you do. I have enjoyed every minute of my research, training, and practice!

It really would have been enough for me to just continue expanding my own career.

My fantastic teachers, mentors, colleagues, and clients have made my life so rich, so interesting, so delightful, and so exciting! I can never repay them for everything they have given me.

But my work always felt incomplete somehow.

I am such a book lover that I naturally assume that the answer to any question lies somewhere in a book. I have an unbelievably, obsessively extensive collection of books on esoteric subjects, especially divination.

For decades I have been waiting for a book about the real work of being an all-around fortune teller, not a con artist but somebody who professionally specialized in the divination arts. I wanted a detailed book that would focus on the business of doing readings in every possible way, a book that would give me little inside tips that would make me more successful, that would guide me to avoid roadblocks and pitfalls.

I longed to find that book before I started reading publicly. I had so many questions! I was afraid of making some really stupid mistakes because I was in such unfamiliar territory. I felt the same way about opening my private office. What in the heck was I doing, anyway? Who did I think I was? Signing that first lease was terrifying.

And doing phone readings for the first time! I think I nearly blacked out.

Performing as a party reader at that first event was a little easier, because my former career was in show business and professional events. As I continued as a party reader, I noticed how difficult presenting at parties appropriately seemed to be for other readers, and I realized it was because they had no idea what their purpose was at the party and how best to present fortune telling in that environment. They would have no idea why the event planner never hired them again. At psychic fairs, I noticed some readers doing much better than others. I was determined to discover why.

As I became more involved in my local tarot community (and a bit later in the international tarot community) I noticed there still was nobody offering answers to the questions I was asking. As I discovered those answers myself, I began helping others.

As those others became wildly successful with the information I gave them, I slowly realized where that darn book was.

Valentina Burton
April 27, 2011
Dallas, Texas

Reading in Public

Twenty-five years ago, I sat enjoying a hot drink in the bar of the famous La Fonda Hotel in Santa Fe, New Mexico.

I was a young actress/performer/producer from Dallas, Texas, who had a secret passion for all forms of divination, especially astrology and tarot.

The lobby bar is enormous at the La Fonda, and it's always busy with little pockets of activity here and there.

I was fascinated with a woman who sat in a quiet corner of the lobby.

She sat at a small table with a drink and a deck of tarot cards. I watched as she read the cards for clients, and then dived into reading a novel between sessions.

I remember thinking how perfect it must be to be her … to spend the days and evenings reading her novel as much as she wished, her only interruption clients requesting the pleasure of a tarot card reading.

Many years later, still secretly passionate about fortune telling, I was booked as a magician to perform at a Christmas party at a large mansion on an estate in the country. After my show was over and I was packed up, I wandered around the mansion to see what other entertainers had been booked and to admire the fabulous decorations.

I stumbled into a long hallway where a line of guests snaked out the door of a bedroom.

What were all these people so excited about that they would wait patiently in the line for an hour? I was stunned to discover it was a tarot card reader! I was even more stunned to discover that she was spending 20 minutes with each guest and her only festive bit of costuming at this very elegant Christmas party was a beat up red beret.

Hmmmm! My brain started ticking away … What If?

What if the fortune teller was in an amazing fabulous theatrical costume?

What if the room the fortune teller was in was decorated to go with her beautiful costume?

What if the fortune teller did readings that were about five minutes long, so guests would not have to wait, and everybody at the party would get a reading?

Shortly after that, I designed and created some lovely gypsy-style fortune teller costumes, made up an exotic name for myself, acquired a pretty, small antique round table, secretly built a super-magnet into the top of the table so I could season my tarot card readings with eerie magic tricks (once a magician, always a magician …), designed how I would do quick party readings, and had photos professionally taken, to send to all the entertainment booking agents.

I did all of this surreptitiously, because I was worried about a potential backlash if the general public discovered I read tarot cards. At this time in my life I was a very successful entertainer in Dallas, Texas. I even had a popular local after-school television show! Dallas is a wonderfully creative city, but it is a very conservative city.

It was probably arrogant of me to believe that anyone would really care about this, but I have always been a cautious person. I wasn't about to sacrifice all I had worked for over so many years in order to create this new, experimental product.

Because I had an excellent reputation with the booking agents, I was able to almost immediately get booked for parties. Having a fortune teller at a private party or a trade show was a new idea and I hit the ground running, solving problems as they came up and designing ever more elaborate costumes and creating themed divination systems.

As the years went by, my work shifted more and more towards fortune telling and away from theatrical magic. (Following my passion, naturally!)

At first I was horrified to discover that people were more interested in what I might tell them about themselves than in the cool magic trick I could do with my tarot cards.

Like many magicians, I assumed that the card or palm reading by itself was not enough, I assumed I needed to jazz it up to make it interesting. Not true!

Guests were so knocked out by the tarot readings that they were too distracted to pay attention to my magic. All they wanted was for me to read for them. This became true even backstage at events, where the other performers and crew demanded I read for them.

One day I received a strange phone call. It was from a man who explained that he owned a hotel near downtown Dallas and was planning a large party for a bunch of friends. I apparently had done a birthday party years before for one of the men who ran the hotel for him, so I came highly recommended, and he really wanted me to read at his party.

I accepted the booking, and when I showed up for the gig the place was utter bedlam.

I was placed at a small round table in the main hallway, under a flashing neon sign. Drunken partiers tripped over me and the noise level was impossible, but I soldiered through the evening, collected my check, and didn't think any more about it.

About a month later the man called me again. He was excited and laughing. Apparently, I had read for some of his best friends, made some outlandish predictions (which they blew off), and then scared the life out of them when those outlandish predictions came true a few weeks later. He couldn't have been happier! He booked me for a few more parties at the hotel, and then one day called me and asked if it was possible for him to hire me to be at the hotel all the time.

I did some thinking and realized that I was still enchanted with the idea of the elegant lady in the hotel lobby bar reading for guests between chapters of her novel.

I decided I wanted to experiment with this, so I contacted him, offering to be there for free to him, working for tips or perhaps charging a small fee to guests as I played with the idea and discovered what worked and what didn't work in reading cards in a hotel lobby.

He was delighted and told me to do it anyway I wanted to do it, just to please be there as much as possible.

For six months I tried every possible location for my table in the lobby; every possible type and size of table; every possible way of presenting the readings; every possible way of managing the "who's next" issue; every possible way of elegantly suggesting that I was not compensated by the hotel, and so I would appreciate remuneration for my readings; every possible way of dealing with the discouragement of doing a 45 minute reading for a client who drove up to the hotel in a Rolls-Royce, exclaimed that my reading was the best he'd ever had, and then handed me a five dollar bill. (Seriously. I am not making this up.)

I ran up against several seemingly insurmountable issues:

It was nearly impossible for me to read cards, manage my list of who's next, go find the next person (who had vanished into the bar and was now drunk), make change for guests, and handle obnoxious and rude people who interrupted me during readings.

I was so frustrated; I was ready to be done with my little experiment. It certainly was not the experience I had expected! I was about as far from the lovely, serene woman I had spotted so many years before at the La Fonda Hotel as it was possible to get.

I had one last idea. What if reading in public really was not a one-person job? I have always had difficulties with delegation, and imagined maybe this was a big lesson for me. I called up David Alexandre, a wonderful lifelong friend who, as an artist, had a very flexible schedule, and I lured him to take a meeting with me by promising him the best crème brûlée in Dallas.

I presented him with the results of my experiment and the problems I was running up against. I asked him if he was interested in attempting to solve these problems and possibly designing something creative, brand-new, and exciting with me. He agreed!

The rest is history, as they say.

David and I have become something of a tourist attraction in Dallas.

People drive and fly in and tell us we are one of the "must do" activities in Dallas these days. I have become the Empire State Building of fortune tellers! How thrilling!

Are You Ready to Read in Public?

Do you think reading in public sounds like fun?

Do you think you have the personality to handle dealing with the frequently funny but also extremely difficult situations that arise for a public reader?

If so, then here are the steps to follow.

How to Find a Good Public Location

Of course, it's the public part of reading in public that is the most difficult.

The question of "where to read" really boils down to choosing your clientele and finding a good location: Who do you want to read for and where do they congregate?

The clientele we experience at Hotel Zaza (and "experience" is the correct word...) is different from the clientele you might find by telling fortunes at a bookstore, coffee shop, restaurant, or bar ... so choose your clientele according to your own interests and comfort.

Locating a venue will depend on your geographical location, and some readers will definitely find their choices limited by geography. It makes a huge difference if you live in a metropolis, out in the country, or in a tourist area that has a seasonal shifting of population.

If you live in an urban area, finding a venue is fairly easy, because you will have many choices. The basic idea to keep in mind is that your venue contact, who is usually the owner or manager of the venue, will have financial goals for the venue. If you can demonstrate that what you will bring to his venue will add to his profits, you will have his attention.

Do not expect most venues to have any sort of budget for entertainment. Every entertainer I have ever met assumes that David and I are handsomely paid by Hotel Zaza to appear there. Although it is a fancy hotel, bar and restaurant, with a celebrity clientele, there is almost no budget for entertainment!

Do your homework before you present your idea to the venue owner or manager. Visit the space at different times and study the clientele, the architectural layout of the venue (is there a quiet and unused space that would be perfect for a reader?), and the menu price points. We have no trouble currently charging $30.00 for a reading at Hotel Zaza because it is at least $20.00 for a glass of wine.

Another tactic is to spend time in the venue. Get to know some of the staff. Be friendly and fun, and tip them well! Owners and managers are usually very hands-on in restaurants, bars, and small hotels. Become a regular patron and one day spontaneously fall into a conversation with the manager about your fascinating occupation as a card reader, and tell him some hilarious stories about your job. Oh, and, by the way, you have a friend and colleague who reads cards regularly at a bar/restaurant/hotel in another city, and has become a huge draw and attraction for the venue, isn't that interesting? Leave the manager with this idea planted, and the next time you see him he will think he has had a brilliant idea and wants to talk you into reading on Friday nights at his bar.

If you live way out in the woods and don't have anything like a luxury resort or dude ranch nearby, you might wish to focus primarily on doing phone readings, but if you are near to some sort of a tourist attraction, seriously consider altering your presentation and mode of divination to fit the theme and look of that venue.

For example, if you live in a rural area near a dude ranch, especially one where corporate events are held on a regular basis, put away your tarot cards and learn a great system for reading playing cards. Order a set of vintage reproduction playing cards to read with and acquire a Victorian Western costume. (Avoid the Miss Kitty saloon gal look, as this is usually too vulgar for corporate events.) Buy a sweet little Victorian table, make a beautiful cloth to go on it, and create some Victorian-looking business cards. On the cards refer to yourself as something like a "prognosticator" or other such 19th century-type verbiage. Create a web page about your new Western Victorian card reader character. Fun stuff!

Find out who organizes the special events for the dude ranch and arrange a short meeting with that person. Take your laptop, playing cards and business cards, but don't dress in costume. Try to look normal and businesslike.

When you meet, show the organizer your adorable web page explaining about the lore of divination in the old West and in the Victorian era. Explain how you are ideal for corporate events because your entertainment is so different, and is always loved by the women and young girls at events, just as it was in the 19th century! Suggest that including you in proposals sent out to corporate clients will show a fresh originality lacking in his competitors.

Do a brief and fun reading for the organizer (and anybody else on site who is interested), and then leave him with some small marketing piece so he will remember you. Remember, his responsibilities and his job rest on his ability to generate a profit for his venue. Show him how you can be a valuable member of his team and add to his bottom line without costing him a penny, and you'll be in.

Find out what the resort is paying (actually, what the corporate client is paying) for musicians and gunslingers; this will give you some idea how to price yourself.

It is really important to select a venue that gets a fair amount of traffic. I have a colleague who read cards for a couple of years in a beautiful, upscale bar-restaurant, but she finally decided to quit because the clientele dwindled to too few and was too boring.

Carefully choose the place you think you want to read in. You will be spending much time there once you get the ball rolling. Aim for venues you think you will enjoy spending time in, with a clientele that amuses you. You will end up knowing everything about everybody there, so select your venue well!

How to Design Your Product

Once you have chosen your venue, you must craft your presentation to fit the space. Hopefully, you have already figured out an ideal area in the location to situate yourself.

Your Table

Find and bring your own reading table. Do not ever use an existing table in a bar or restaurant. Why not? In the first place, a table is valuable moneymaking real estate for the venue and someone will resent you for taking up space there. Second, if you are a female and you are reading cards in a bar, sitting alone for an extended period of time at the bar or at one of the bar tables several nights a week will send the wrong message about your occupation.

Look at the decor in the venue and find, purchase, or make table coverings and props that coordinate with it. This is not the time to be cheap. Make your table look even nicer than the décor. Have a pretty little sign professionally made for your table with your name, what you are offering, and the price.

Your Clothing

Dress yourself to fit the venue. A brief time spent online researching costume history will enable you to coordinate your costume to the era and the regional style of the architecture and furniture in the venue. Choose things to wear that go well with the look of your table and that will be attractive to the existing clientele in the venue.

If you are a female reader, you have many choices that will complement the decor of your venue. In a very modern space you might choose outfits that are sleek and modern and simple: think Audrey Hepburn. A charming mid-century space might call for something more like Elizabeth Montgomery in "Bewitched." A kooky Bohemian space will allow for lots of fringe and patterns, and you can go completely Stevie Nicks with your wardrobe.

If you are a male reader, avoid looking either sleazy or New Agey, although sleazy is probably preferable to nerdy. Unless the venue is Bohemian, the gypsy dude look doesn't work, and neither does the ponytailed hippie dude look. Leave your Renaissance Faire costume at home, unless your public venue actually is a Ren Faire. For most venues, classic, elegant, and not too casual is the way to go if you are a man. Think of how appealing and intriguing it would be to venture out to an elegant bar or restaurant and come across a male tarot card reader who was well groomed, dressed like Cary Grant, and seemed friendly, interesting, knowledgeable, and fun. Would you choose to get a reading from him? I certainly would! Probably every woman I know would!

Standing Out From the Clientele

What does all of this nonsense about tablecloths and clothing have to do with tarot card reading? If the clientele who frequent the venue does not think that you look interesting, charming, and fun, they will not even venture to inquire about your card reading. It won't matter if you are the greatest tarot card reader in the world; if potential clients are not moved to get a reading by what they see of you, all of that greatness is wasted, and another opportunity to show how tarot is amazing and exciting is lost.

Overcoming the Reluctance of the Clientele

If you read in public you are an ambassador for all of the divination arts and you need to take that seriously. Many of those you read for will be having their first experience of any kind of reading with you.

The general public has two negative assumptions about getting a tarot card reading:

First, they may think that the reading will be a general, cold-reading-cookie-cutter cliché; t,hat it will be stupid, boring, and a waste of time and money.

Second, they are afraid that the reading will freak them out and ruin their whole evening by revealing a terrible, embarrassing secret!

Either of these assumptions can block potential clients from getting a reading at a public venue, so part of your job is to do anything you can to subtly illustrate that the client's experience will not be stupid, boring, a waste of time, scary, or embarrassing.

Once you have developed a reputation and a clientele in a public venue most of these problems are solved, because you will have returning clients and plenty of word of mouth business. Until that time, you must deal with this gracefully.

The Amount of Time to Offer Per Reading

Your actual reading in a public setting should probably not be longer than 20 minutes.

It's important not to keep clients away from the bar too long … the manager wants them to keep ordering drinks, and their friends want to visit with them.

I usually structure my hotel readings to have two layouts of cards.

The first layout is a quick look at the next six months for the client. It will briefly touch on everything in their life, as well as cover the theme and main issues going on.

The second layout is to answer any question they may have. It sometimes takes a while for the client to choose a question, so I frequently suggest subjects for the question and sometimes will re-word the question.

I go very fast, so I like for the clients to record the session. Almost everybody I see has a smart phone and they record beautifully.

If clients have lots of questions, you can hand them a card and ask them to make an appointment at your private office. You can even write a code word on the back of your business card, tell them to call you for an appointment and give you the code, and you can give them a full-length office visit for $70.00 instead of $100.00 — that is, for the difference between your public reading price and a private session.

How to Price Your Readings

Always have a price for your readings. Do not read for tips.

Reading for tips always left me feeling frustrated and unappreciated, but it took me a long time to learn that setting up my public readings so that clients tipped me as payment also made my clients very uncomfortable and left them feeling nervous. This is because people have no idea how much to tip a tarot or palm reader for a reading.

Honestly, most people still have trouble with how much to tip a waiter or cab driver, so how can you expect even the most sophisticated client to have a clue when it comes to how much of a tip will be appropriate for you, the fortune teller?

Reading for tips simply doesn't work. Set a price and stick to it. Create readings that are so good that your clients almost always tip on top of the price of the reading.

How should you price your readings?

A good rule in bars or restaurants is to price the reading at twice the price of a drink. Our readings at Hotel Zaza are $30.00, and most clients will hand us two twenties. Cocktails at Zaza are around $15.00 and a glass of wine is $20.00.

We will occasionally get a few "tire-kickers" who say $30.00 is too much, but these are usually people we are not interested in reading for anyway, so we will mysteriously smile and agree that obviously this is not the right time for them to get a reading.

The mysterious smile technique defuses the situation elegantly.

The subtext to their offer is that your service is not worth $30.00, and you are just a money grubbing cheap fortune teller, so of course you will read their cards for 20 bucks.

Your response reveals that you do not need their money, and actually find them not very interesting. Because you are smiling, and saying things that seem to have their best interests at heart they cannot take offense, yet you have remained in control of the situation.

You must remember that the clients are extremely lucky to have the opportunity to get a reading from you. They are not doing you a favour by handing you that little bit of cash; you are doing them a favour by being available.

Your Wrangler

Use a wrangler.
I repeat: use a wrangler!

Inevitably, you will find yourself in a situation while reading in public, where you're dealing with an out-of-control jerk. This usually will not be a client you are reading for, just somebody walking past your table who feels the need to abuse you.

A horrible man who was incredibly, relentlessly verbally abusive to me at the Hotel Zaza was one of the things that finally motivated me to ask David to be my wrangler.

It's your wrangler's job to steer the jerk away from your table and alert Security if the fool won't take the hint.

Also, when reading for attractive female clients, you will witness an amazing phenomenon. Any dudes in the bar who were too intimidated to approach her earlier in the evening will now see a golden opportunity to plop down beside her at your table and announce that the tall dark handsome stranger in the cards has arrived. (Ah! So witty!)

Your wrangler will remove the offending idiot so you can continue your reading.

A wrangler also helps you set up and tear down your table, handles the money, keeps a list of who's next, gives you the visual signals that help you time your readings efficiently, refills your water glass, reminds you to go to the bathroom, and drives home with you at two o'clock in the morning so you are safer.

David and I borrowed the name "wrangler" from our theatrical background: A wrangler is used on a movie set to manage children or animals. We thought it was hilariously appropriate.

I pay all of my wranglers 25% of the gross. They truly are worth so much more!

Potential Disaster

David and I were at the hotel one evening. Prior to going in, he received a call to book an appointment for a woman named Rachel and her friends.

We set up as usual. Within minutes, two women walked up and said they were here for their reading. David asked them their names and one of them replied: "Mary and Rachel."

David sat them at our table and went to the bar to get our coffees and check with the restaurant hostess for any inquiries. The hostess referred him to a group of ladies at the bar who had expressed an interest earlier and he approached them to see if they were still interested. One woman took him aside and gave him a long list of names and ended the list with the name Rachel.

David, of course, put it together that there had been a mix up and the first ladies were walk-ups, and this group was the one with the reservation. Still, he thought no harm, no foul, all is right with the world and no one would be the wiser. (Famous last words!)

David returned to the table and about ten minutes into the current reading was approached by two women rushing in from outside who breathlessly announced, "Sorry we're late, we got here as fast as we could!" Somewhat confused by this, he asked: "Did you make an appointment?" The woman, with a distinctly aggravated tone, said, "I'm Rachel and I called earlier."

You could have knocked David over with a feather! The sheer amount of ass kissing, bowing and scraping necessary to avoid total disaster in this situation has put David in the category of legendary in the world of wranglers. Almost everyone got their readings that night and left happy. It was a miracle.

The one aspect of this that is not forgotten, however, is: Always, Always, Always, make sure you get as much info as possible from clients, such as last name and cell number! Stay organized in your dealings with people. Use helpful tricks like notes about their appearance and the location where they will be waiting, written down.

If the staff at your venue has any ability to assist you they usually will, but do not rely on them to keep you organized! As an independent contractor you should develop a system that supports you in being autonomous.

You must never be a burden to the people who work around you, and you must always assume that everyone named Rachel will show up all at the same time for a reading.

Reading at Parties

For a professional reader, parties are, in my opinion, a fantastic way to improve your skills at divination, to pop out of bad habits you might get into doing private readings, and to have some fun with the image of a "Reader."

Some people have the idea that it is possible to make an amazing amount of money performing at parties as a psychic tarot reader. However, although it is possible to make some money, parties are nearly always on Friday or Saturday nights and so are limited by that constraint.

Parties also involve a great deal of preparation and set up, so I have found it impossible to schedule a private session within two or three hours of party start time.

Ask yourself: "Even though I might make $300.00, $400.00, or $500.00 at a party, could I have scheduled two or three private client sessions during the time I was preparing for, performing at, and returning home from the party?"

Yes, you could!

So, private parties are not the wonderful cash cow that many who have not ever done a party imagine them to be!

When you decide to offer your services as entertainment for private parties, you are competing with magicians, caricature artists, disc jockeys, hula dancers, and musicians.

You are also competing with the caterer for a slice of the budget for the entire party.

If your marketing materials do not reflect knowledge of party and event dynamics, and a comprehension of the needs of your clients, you will not get booked.

The Party Client

A potential client calling you about a party does not have the same needs as a client calling you for a private reading.

What does a party client want?

A party client wants to have a party that the guests talk about months after the event.

A party client wants to be able to have fun at her own party and not have to manage minutiæ at the event.

A party client wants to impress her guests with her chic, her intelligence, and her sophistication.

A party client wants to have this fabulous party but have it be easy for her.

In truth, she wants all of these things much more than she wants something cheap! (Remember that!)

So, what is the product you are actually selling to your party and event clients?

You are selling a service that provides fun, excitement, sophistication, and a personal touch (since you are doing personal readings for each guest).

You are also selling your experience, expertise, and professionalism. This expertise and professionalism gives your client (the host or party planner) a degree of serenity.

That is what your client really wants.

The party client could very easily go to a college campus or a coffee shop and find someone reading tarot cards who would be delighted to read at the party for "the big bucks," but that is not all she wants. The client is also fearful of hiring a flaky person who will
  • Show up late
  • Not show up at all
  • Show up drunk or stoned
  • Be weird, and not in an amusing way …

When you understand who your party client is, what she wants and what she does not want, it is not difficult to create a great party experience for her.

One mistake I see frequently see made by private readers who attempt to do parties is the tendency to get stuck in what the reader wants, not what the client wants.
  • A private party is not a counseling session.
  • A private party is not an appropriate place to discuss the history of tarot, divination, spirituality, or religion.
  • A private party is not the place to recruit new clients for your private practice.
  • A private party is not an appropriate place to find your next boyfriend.

You will find many party guests who are interested in what you do and may want to know more about it. It is appropriate to have business cards or any sort of small card detailing your public appearances, meetups, blogs, website, and classes to hand to them — that is, unless the party or event is booked through an agent! Never hand out any sort of promotional materials at an event that has been booked by a party professional.

Your time is almost always very limited with each person at a private party, and you cannot spend that time on anything other than doing readings as quickly as possible. You are responsible for managing this! The guests will usually be drinking and in a party mood, they are not thinking about the management of your time, that is your job!

David and I nearly always work with a wrangler at parties, public events, and special events. The wrangler's job is to help set up the reader's table, manage the guests, act as a bouncer if necessary, manage the time, manage the money if we are charging a fee per reading, and make sure the reader has water, bathroom breaks, etc.

Why Read at Parties?

I began this chapter detailing what I believe to be the benefits of doing private parties. Making a lot of money is not one of them. The overhead and the time consumed by the party does not justify the little extra cash you will make.

So, why do them?
I mentioned three benefits to you in the first sentence of this chapter:
  • Improve skills
  • Break bad habits
  • Play with the image

Improve Your Skills

The first reason to work at parties is to improve your skills as a reader.

When you have 50 people at a party, and four hours to do a short reading for each one of them — a reading that leaves each of them happy, amused, and satisfied — you must be more organized with your reading. You must have rehearsed a layout that will take no longer than two or three minutes to read.

I recommend practicing, timing yourself (with an actual timer!) to make sure you are quick and efficient. If you practice enough, you will be able to feel when you have spent three minutes on the reading.

In three minutes you cannot detail someone's life or go very deeply into the issues they face. (You can see these issues; you just cannot go there….) This is a good thing! The last thing you want is to have a party guest burst into tears or be so riveted by what you say that she will not get out of the chair.

Practice with the short layout you have chosen. Practice what you will say and come up with short, pithy, funny readings of the cards in question. Please remember that, in the party venue, you are an entertainer and not a counsellor.

The cards have many layers of meaning: Choose the meanings that are amusing and fun. How does this improve your skills as a reader? It forces you to have some discipline and also to see the cards in a new way. It places constraints upon you of time, energy, and focus.

Returning to doing full private sessions after a private party or a corporate trade show always feels exciting and fresh. The cards themselves feel like they have had a vacation and are ready to speak in a new way.

Break Bad Habits

How can reading at parties break bad habits created by doing only private sessions?

One of the wonderful things about doing private sessions is that people seek you out, usually on the referral of others who are extremely happy with your work, and they are pleased and excited to be able to have time with you. They will take notes; they will record the session, and in many ways they will hang on your every golden word.

Gee it's awesome!

And all of that awesomeness conceals a trap. It is extremely easy to begin to believe that you are Amazing, you are the Oracle!

The arrogance that can develop from this is the downfall of many fine readers. The bad habit I am speaking of is a habit of thinking of yourself as Super Spiritual, a Spiritual Superstar!

When you do a party, the guests are not there to worship you. The guests are there to have a good time. Performing at parties as an entertainer will keep you humble, and that is a very good thing.

A dear friend of mine showed up for a gig at a large mansion a few years ago.

She was feeling very glamorous in an exquisite silk costume as she rang the doorbell.

The hostess answered and exclaimed "Oh, thank God you're here! Can you work an extra hour? The performing monkey we hired is not able to show up tonight."

Play With the Image

When you're booked for a party or a corporate event, many times the party or event will have a theme. This is an opportunity to create something wonderful for the guests and to tie in what you do thematically. You can re-invent yourself for each party!

Even if there is no theme and the party client says, "Just show up wearing anything; it's just casual," don't do it! When clients say that, they are simply not imaginative enough to think of some way you could be presented well. And, actually, it is not their job to figure this out for you. Yes, you could just run over to the party in your jeans and sweater. Nobody will say anything. Nobody will seem to care. However, you will not be seen as special, unusual, unique, and offering value above and beyond. They will like you, but they will not remember you. A party is Show Business, and in show business not being memorable is death.

Is it more work to be fabulous? Yes!

Is it worth it? Yes!

Decide on your "Look." If you need help, find a good friend (or hire a professional!) to act as a stylist for you. Always be elegant, even if you are putting together something over-the-top. Please leave behind any political, alternative religion, or lifestyle symbols. Nobody cares what you do in your private life, and they really don't want to know.

Leave behind clichés also. A broomstick skirt, a caftan, or a wolf T-shirt impresses no one. Dump the comfy hippie sandals unless you are creating a Vintage Hippie character. Try to find the distinction between Mysterious and Negative. (Hint: choose Mysterious!)

Ramp up the glamour!

You are the Mysterious Fortune Teller to the client and guests: Be that!

I shouldn't have to say this, because it seems so obvious, but you must never smoke, drink alcohol, or eat at a party, corporate event, or trade show. Do not drink alcohol before the gig, either. You will want to have something to drink at your table so you don't lose your voice, but choose something that won't give you stinky breath. Be religious about managing your breath! You can look fantastic and be the most amazing party reader in the world, but if that client sits down and is repelled by your breath, you lose.

You might want to consider pulling the fearsome-looking cards out of your deck before you read at a party. This is controversial, but your job at the party is to entertain. Many of the guests at these functions have never had a card reading, and the macho ones who are so offhand and jokey about it are secretly pretty scared of what you might say. Paring down your deck for party venues will not keep the cards from being truthful and clear, but it will prevent you from getting bogged down in explaining a frightening-looking card to an impressionable guest, or having an important client receive an unfortunate message!

In response to those who feel that theatricalizing tarot reading or offering psychic divination at a party or corporate trade show demeans our sacred art in some way, I can only suggest that performing with our best talents and skills in such a venue allows more contact with the general public, and is a great opportunity to do some positive public relations for our field of endeavour. Let's be honest: Our field really needs a PR makeover! The general public tends to think of us as arrogant, nerdy, and boring, or they are convinced that we are all creepy con artists, so anything that can sway them to see us as charming, funny, entertaining, sophisticated, and interesting is a plus. I know this is more work, I know we shouldn't have to do this, but we do.

How to Book a Party

I have a high rate of success booking private parties, due to my years working in the party and event business.

As I said before, the key is to always remember what the client wants, and then to give it to her! When she calls you to inquire about your services, she will be a little nervous. You must answer the phone and be warm and engaging. She has probably never spoken to someone like you before! Be relaxed, warm, and funny.

Rehearse a brief script about how you read at parties.

Tell the client that you will show up ahead of party time with your wrangler to set up your table and area, and then the two of you will vanish until your scheduled start time. That way her guests will not be treated to the vision of you dragging in your table and unpacking your case.

Tell her that when it is time for you to begin, you can either make a grand entrance and announce your presence to the assembled guests, or your wrangler can simply sign up everyone as you begin the first reading.

Tell her that unless it is a small dinner party, you will do readings for each guest that are from three to seven minutes long, and your wrangler will manage the time and have the next guest ready to go as you complete each reading.

Tell her that you will divide the number of guests into the number of minutes she has booked you, and that this will determine how long each reading needs to be.

Some clients will try to get you to reduce your fee by suggesting that they can supply someone to be your wrangler, or by saying that they had already planned to simply have a sign-up sheet at the party, and that is all you will need. Party planners are notorious for suggesting this. Don't fall for it!

Sign-up sheets and untrained wranglers will only work if everybody at the party is sober all night and the guests enjoy standing in line. Trust me; your untrained wrangler will mysteriously vanish just when things get really hairy! It will be impossible to teach this unknown person to cue you silently about the timing on readings, to trust them to have a sense of urgency about having the next guest lined up and ready to go as you finish each reading, to get them to pay attention to refilling your water glass, and to train them about how to manage the inevitable "reading hog" guest, who thinks they get to have a thirty minute reading at a private party.

Stand your ground firmly about bringing your own wrangler. You are a professional.

This is a great point in the conversation to ask the client about the details of her party. How many guests? What is the venue? What are the other activities at the party? What is the theme/colour or scheme/reason for the party?

Your potential client will be very impressed with your attention to detail and professionalism. She will realize that she is in very good hands and you will not need any of her attention during her party. At this point, she is probably wishing that her caterer was as organized as you are!

Pricing for Parties

The client will be worried about the cost of all this fabulousness, so let her know the price and Never, Ever discount your price to anyone, EVER. The folks who finagle a discount from you will be more trouble than they are worth.

Do not ever believe a whiny hard luck story from somebody calling to book you for a party! You will show up and find they live in a five million dollar mansion, have hired a famous pop singer, and have the best chef in town catering in the kitchen. It is very common to discover that the client who has paid less for you also has put you right next to the noisy DJ or outside on a freezing porch, and acts resentful about giving you a glass of water or showing you where the bathroom is.

Even if I do not have a party booked on a given Saturday night, I will never accept a last-minute engagement from somebody who tells me that I should accept less because I am available and I "might as well make the money." I feel that they should pay more, not less, as an aggravation fee for booking me at the last minute.

Do not have different prices for different classes of people, parts of town, etc.

If you feel like you have to change your price and negotiate with the client, or do things to boost your price in some way, you need to raise your fee!

Trust me on this: The more you charge, the more respect you will have from your client. To do your best work, you need to feel that your client is delighted and excited to have you at her party — and any sort of disrespectful behaviour from the client creates a nasty little lump of resentment that is hard to shake off.

What should the fee be for a fortune teller at a party?

Obviously, there will be regional differences in price, but the easiest way to calculate an appropriate price is to look at the fees charged in your area by magicians and other adult party entertainers. Research the fees charged by the top entertainers in your area. don't mess with the low-ball folks. There will always be entertainers who attempt to stay booked based on low price, but they never last long in the business, so ignore them. You do not have to charge a fee as high as the top entertainers in your area, but you should probably be just a little below that.

Look at how those entertainers handle their bookings. Do they require a deposit? What do they charge for out-of-town gigs? How do they answer the phone?

The successful entertainers in your area have already invented the wheel; they have already solved many of the problems you would run into.

Also, call and talk to a few of these entertainers and tell them what you are planning to do. Many of them, especially DJs, frequently book other entertainers and will love to know about what you are doing so they can book you! If they have time, they can give you valuable advice on the local market and what you can expect from booking parties.

Many clients just assume that a tarot reader is flaky and disorganized. They will be delighted when you handle your business with integrity.

It's very important to keep all communications professional and clear. Always have some sort of letter of agreement for all party engagements, even ones you may not be paid for, such as charity events.

I have discovered through trial and error that collecting a nonrefundable deposit for every party I book is a really good idea, as it cuts down on the frivolous folks who will book me on a whim and then cancel at the last minute, after I have turned down other engagements for the same evening.

I have also discovered that clients frequently want the reader to do an hour or two of overtime at the conclusion of a party. These clients usually have more guests than they expected and are being pressured by their guests to keep the reader at the party to read for everyone. Always include an overtime form in your suitcase; and be sure to have the hostess sign off on any overtime you agree to do, especially if she has been drinking! If you do not, she will not remember after the party what she agreed to, and this can be a sticky situation.

It is always best to collect cash or a check for the balance due to you at the party. If you have to process a credit card the week after the party, you frequently will play phone tag (sometimes for weeks!) with the client, plus pay exorbitant credit card processing fees.

A dear friend and colleague of mine is trying to convince me to only do gigs where I collect the entire fee up front with a credit card. She does this with her entertainment company and she swears that her system weeds out the difficult, high maintenance clients. I am not brave enough to ask for this yet, but I know I will soon!

Pay attention to how you feel about charging for entertaining at a party. If you feel a pang of guilt, like, "Well, I'm just starting out, so I really should work for free a few times or should charge $20.00 an hour because I'm so new to this," you need to work on yourself before you attempt to market yourself as a party fortune teller!

Working for free or a low rate says to the general public that you do not value divination, or your talents and gifts, and so they are right to marginalize you. (And that allows them to marginalize tarot and tarot readers in general!)

Party Readings to Go

If you want to read at parties, I recommend that you get a piece of luggage, such as a suitcase with wheels, that remains always packed and ready to go with a basic party set up:
- A spare set of your favourite tarot cards (if you are card reading)
- Your business cards
- A lovely small notebook and pen for your wrangler
- Mints, breath spray, and hand wipes
- Emergency over-the-counter pain medication
- An energy drink
- A pretty and unobtrusive cup or mug for your drink on your table
- Some beautiful fabrics to cover your table
- Candles and candlesticks as props
- A crystal ball (to read or as a prop)

Fabrics

Visit an Indian import store and stock up on saris. Saris have between 6 and 8 yards of fabric, come in every price range, and are lushly, exotically beautiful. To begin, purchase two different deep red saris, and a shawl or throw, also in red. The shades of red can be different, as combining them looks very rich. Later, you can expand to other sets of colours.

Your Business Cards

Business cards are a must; you simply will not be seen as a professional without a good business card. Do not use business cards printed with a computer printer, they are too thin and look too amateurish. Find a good printer who will print up cards on heavy stock. I recommend having a good photo of yourself on the card, along with your name, phone number, and maybe a couple of bullet points about what you do. It is fine to put your professional email address on your card but never, never include your home address.

David and I have played with different kinds of cards over the years and we keep coming back to cards printed on heavy stock with a signature colour and our photos and phone number.

People who ask for your business card will hang onto it, sometimes for years, and then refer you to a friend. Business cards are a long-term marketing tool because it is rare that the person picking up your business card will immediately call you.

Party Protocol

If you are booked at a party by another entertainer, an agent, or an event planner, you must never, ever hand out your own marketing materials, including your business cards. Do not even tell guests how to find your website. If you forget and violate this professional rule, the agent or events person who booked you will find out and never book you again.

The person who booked you is jealously guarding the client's information (and even the client's guests' information!), is making a commission on top of your fee, and will get very pissy if it seems you are inserting yourself to steal clients. The client database is the source of the events planner's livelihood. Please remember this or you will get yourself in trouble!

Occasionally, parties will have an event coordinator and a separate entertainment agent. The event coordinator manages the entire party, deals with the caterers, the decor people, and the entertainment agent. In these cases, you must refer any inquiry about you and your services to the lead party professional. Remember the chain of command: Refer inquiring guests to the event coordinator, the party professional at the top of the chain of command, not to the entertainment agent to whom you report and from whom you receive your check.

Party Props

Add to your luggage some metal or wooden candlesticks (never resin or pottery, they always get broken), hanging lanterns, and a crystal ball with a stand. Please select elegant, high quality looking props. Cheap looking is never good! David and I are constantly combing estate sales and antique shops for interesting items for our tables. Gorgeous does not always equal expensive! The most beautiful candelabra I own was only $30.00.

A Word About Candlesticks

Resin candlesticks are very common and easy to find at hobby and discount stores. They will always, always get broken in your luggage.

Resist the urge to purchase resin candlesticks. Some of them look wonderful, but they are not worth the trouble. I wish I had back all the hours I have spent gluing and repairing these fragile objects. Only purchase metal or wooden candlesticks, period.

A Word About Candles

Several years ago David and I had the Dallas Fire Marshal unexpectedly show up and give us a very expensive fine for having lit candles on our table at an event. Ever since then, we have purchased high quality pillar candles and hollowed them out. At events or at the Hotel Zaza, we will insert an electronic candlelight. These are available at any party store and are very cheap. Many of them actually flicker, and look exactly like a real flame. By doing this, our table still looks beautiful but we are now safe from any potential candle related mishap (or hefty fine!).

Problems with candles are more likely to involve wax issues than setting something on fire. Packing up after a party used to take me much longer, because I had to wait for the liquid wax in the candles to set up before packing them away. I spent many years living in terror of dribbling wax on a priceless antique in a beautiful home, but only twice did I actually set my costume on fire by leaning too close to my candles at a corporate event!

Your Crystal Ball

We frequently do take actual crystal balls to our parties. David and I also are always on the lookout for nice poured-glass balls for our party tables. (Yet another excuse for Fun At Estate Sales! You can find beautiful glass ball paperweights that are perfect.)

If you take a real crystal ball to a party you will run the risk of it being dropped. I once had drunken guests at a horrible suburban party grab my Brazilian crystal ball and play catch with it until it smashed to the floor and bounced a few times. I still use that ball for parties, as part of it broke off, conveniently creating a flat base on one side, but the experience was terrible. Always realize that everything on your table is constantly at risk of being bumped, jostled, spilled on, picked up, or played with.

At our Hotel, there is the drama of a fistfight near my table every couple of months or so. When this happens, I scoop the ball and candles off of the table and drop them into a bag waiting beneath the table, while continuing to read for my client. I'm so used to it, I don't miss a beat. (The clients usually find this astonishing and incredibly funny.)

Your Table

After years of my trying to find the best possible table for readings, David discovered a lightweight, cheap, and easy-to-find solution.

I rarely use round tables because it is hard to make props look pretty on them, so my table was a heavy wooden one, roughly 4' x 2'. With this size of rectangular table, you are face-to-face with your client, there is plenty of room for the cards, and an arrangement of candlesticks and crystal ball on one or both sides of the reader looks awesome! I loved my table because it was so stable and I had been using it at Hotel Zaza for years, but it weighed a ton.

When David began as my wrangler, he immediately started looking for a more lightweight version of my beloved table, and found one at, of all places, the local home improvement store! At the time I am writing this, these little plastic tables with folding metal legs cost about $30.00. They are extremely stable and the legs have a mechanism to lock them when they are extended. I can arrive at a party to set up with my rolling suitcase in one hand and my folding table in the other, and not break a sweat!

Your Location at the Party

Your location at a party is of prime importance, and this matter should be discussed between you and the client during the initial conversation you have with her.

It is the tendency for clients to want to place the reader right in the middle of the party. Especially if you are in a fabulous costume and look amazing, the client will want to use you as decor for the party. There are two problems with this:

First, regardless of what people may say, they really do not want others to overhear their reading. The guests will be secretly terrified that you will reveal some deep dark secret out loud. I very rarely will do readings where all of the guests can listen.

The second issue has to do with noise. The middle of the party is usually very noisy. Even if there is not a DJ or a band, the level of conversational ambient noise in the main room of a party makes it very hard to be heard by the guest you are reading for. If you have to stop and repeat yourself four times, your reading time per guest will be significantly longer, and your client will get angry with you for taking too long with each guest and making the other guests wait too long.

There is nothing quite as horrible as being hoarse and exhausted from screaming at the top of your lungs for hours and then having your client and her guests disappointed because you didn't do what you said you would do, because not everybody got a reading at the party.

Yes, this is your problem and not your client's problem. You are a professional, and as such you need to have set good boundaries and organize how you function at a party with grace.

I always require that the client locate me in a library, breakfast room, spare bedroom, large coat closet, or even out in the foyer or the entrance to a ballroom. I will not accept gigs where I am placed in a non-advantageous location.

Sometimes clients will contact you in the belief that having a fortune teller at the party is a great fun idea, but they will then tell you they are worried that it makes people too uncomfortable! If this comes up, offer the client the possibility of you giving a short, light-hearted public presentation of some kind before you begin the private readings.

For instance, for a small dinner party, tell the client that you can make a little presentation after cocktails in the dining room about what fortune tellers do, explaining your work in an amusing way, or offer to give a humorous astrological presentation about the guest of honour. Reassure the client that after the presentation, you will then move into an adjoining area or room to do the short, private readings for each guest.

You Are an Entertainer

The infusion of fabulousness and theatrics at a party or event creates an outstanding environment for tarot to shine.

For me personally, making sure the experience of divination is fun and cool for everyone at an event, by managing it well, is my way of showing commitment to this art form, and respect and appreciation for all my clients.

Rehearse how you will read at a party; design and put together your wardrobe, table, and set up; create a website and marketing materials. There is nothing like preparation to give you confidence!

Create a wonderful product, charge a fair price for it, and go make wonderful things happen in the world!

An Interview with David Alexandre, A Party Reader

Val: David, you have been so successful with party and event readings, what do you think are the necessary ingredients to set up and manage well as a party reader?

David: I would say the primary ingredient is to be aware of the client's expectation. Before you even begin to plan your setup and what you will do, you must be as clear as possible on how the client sees the event. The party is about something or serves some purpose. Is it a birthday? A baby shower? An anniversary? You need to know that and then figure out how to best support the reason for the event. It is likely to have a colour scheme. You need to be consistent with the environment; don't show up with a blue tablecloth for a pink bachelorette party. You need to know what they are expecting. That is the minimum!

Next, let them know that if they don't have an area for you, many of the guests won't realize that you are even there, they will breeze by you and not know what you are doing. They might think you are just another party guest. Make sure you are positioned well in the party. You need a quiet area, so that you aren't screaming all night over a band or loud karaoke, or next to something messy that could splatter all over you and make a mess, or knock over your table. The best is to be cornered off, in an area where it is relatively quiet, where you can be part of the decor but still able to talk to the guests and be heard clearly.

Val: Do you have any tips about transport and management of props, fabric, and tables?

David: You need a handful of wheeled suitcases, They will save your life! If you have a nice stash of props and fabrics, you need to keep them inventoried. I like to use plastic tubs and keep them in a designated spot. Don't have your stuff loose and running around all over your house; it can become a nightmare finding things when you need them. Organize!

Bring your own table, if you can. It should be a lightweight but stable folding table, with locking legs. I did a party the other night where I had to use a shaky table provided by the venue; I spent the entire event worried the table would suddenly collapse. Hotel tables are just beaten to death, and are usually incredibly wobbly. Use your own table and worry less.

I prefer a four-legged table, two-foot by four-foot . It has room for props, cards, or other divination tools, and you are only two feet away from your clients, so they can hear you.

Val: How can someone without a background in design create an area that looks good?

David: Theme it out completely. You want to layer your fabrics. Even if only a tiny bit of each fabric shows, use at least three fabrics. Make it look rich and textured.

Don't buy cheap stuff! Don't use just little glass votives, buy nice candlesticks.

Use real things, not plastic items, never use anything cheap. Spend some money on this stuff. It will last a very long time, and it is a part of your working tools.

Val: What many readers may not know about is how to compose a table, how to arrange props to look really good when you set up. You are really just fantastic at that, and you make it look so easy! Any advice?

David: Most people have a clichéd idea of a fortune teller: A round table, a tablecloth, a candlestick, and a crystal ball. I prefer two candlesticks and three tablecloths.

Use more than one crystal ball. They reflect and bounce light, and they look rich and interesting. Plus, it's a great excuse to collect crystal balls. I use the glass ones, so it's not tragic if a guest drops one. When people walk up, you want them blown away, they can't be all jaded and dismissive, like, "Oh, big deal, a candlestick and a cheap crystal ball."

Use really good replica antique pieces, so you create a wonderful look, but aren't nervous about your $4,000.00 candelabra. Never have your candlesticks the same height. Use a small box under the fabric to elevate one of them.

Put the crystal balls at different levels with electronic tea lights behind them to light them up. Use odd numbers of objects. Never do less. Always add more. As long as you have room for your hands to lay out your cards, the other real estate on that table should be interesting, like a movie set. Do more, not less. Tell a visual story with it.

Val: What are the most common party themes? If someone is just beginning to do this, what would you suggest they gather as a sort of initial supply of themed props?

David: You need a very good-looking Halloween setup, of course. Another popular theme is Gypsy, with bright fabrics, candlesticks, lanterns, a largish crystal ball. Palmistry hands and vintage props are good. Mardi Gras has become a popular theme year-round.

Val: Yes, I remember one Christmas where nearly every party had a Mardi Gras theme! It was so funny!

9

David: Yes, and that year we didn't do any parties with a Mardi Gras theme during Mardi Gras! Very strange.

One last piece of advice: Do a dry run of your setup at home, a week before the event. Take a photo of it and email it to your client! They will either be very impressed that you are so thorough, or they may say they had a different idea, and you will now have time to get more clear about their expectation.

Val: Back to expectation!

David: Yes! Just showing up and hoping they will like what you have chosen and how you have put it together is risky. Just a little more effort and communication can put your work on a whole other level.

Val: Yes, I agree. Thank you so much!

Propriety

Near the end of a very long evening at the hotel, David seats the last client, an attractive young woman. I ask her what question she would like the cards to answer. She loudly replies, "Tell me about Brian Smith!"

I examine the layout, and there's plenty of Magician reversed, Seven of Swords, Three of Swords. You get the idea!

I'm too tired to pull any punches, so I launch into my interpretation of the cards.

"He's a real sleaze ball." She seems amused, and oddly disinterested, just giggling a bit. I continue with, "If he is a romantic interest, you are not the only gal he's currently seeing."

At this precise moment, David realizes that not only is "Brian Smith" her date, but he is sitting directly behind her and listening, and becoming very agitated.

Before the next card is read, the guy springs up from his chair and heads for the bar.

Meanwhile, I ramble on. I tell her he's being shady in his financial dealings.

As I discover later, he returned from the bar, walked by the table and leaned in for a listen, just as I blurted out, "… and he has a strange relationship with his mother!"

That's when I notice David becoming manic in his gestures, nervously fiddling with the candles on the table. He sees what's happening, but can't think of a way to stop me. The Train Has Left The Station.

Repeatedly, each time "Brian" cruises past the table he gets another earful.

The girl is giggling, and I'm not sure what to think of that, so I wrap up the reading and she leaves.

Because he knows I'll be mortified, David doesn't tell me the full story until we're out in the car on the way home. I am mortified. For weeks.

We have since created a secret code that cautions of a potentially explosive situation, or, in other words, to get me to shut up.

Conly
Boston

Reading in Your Office

There comes a point in the career of every professional psychic when the big question comes up: "Where can I privately read for clients?"

Some readers call the private space in which they give one-on-one readings a "parlour," while others know it as an "office," a "temple," a "church," or even a "shop."

The word "parlour" evokes the historical image of a reader who sees clients in the front parlour of a home, but in current usage, it can refer to any sort of private reading space.

The term "office" suggests that the space is definitely not located at the reader's home. A "temple" or "church" implies an emphasis on ministerial credentials.

The word "shop" indicates that, in addition to readings, the fortune teller also offers occult curios, candles, and books for sale at the site.

For simplicity's sake, I will call all of these private reading venues "offices."

When is it Time to Find Your Own Office?

For me, the decision to find my own space came when I was overwhelmed with clients from Hotel Zaza who wanted private readings.

Some of these people were pretty pushy and insisted that it would be a great idea to come to my house so I could read for them. Others were insistent about the idea of house calls, wanting me to drive over and read for them in their homes.

I found both of these ideas pretty terrifying.

I was not about to go driving around all over North Texas, trying to find an address in order to read for a client for an hour. What a crazy waste of time!

I toyed briefly with the idea of blocking off the front living room and dining room of my home and making it my fortune teller parlour. (I thought this was a particularly charming and old-fashioned idea!) However, at the time I had a teenage son and a whole bunch of rowdy mixed-breed rescue dogs, which were all just too noisy and intrusive to make the reading-in-my-home plan anything other than a potential disaster for me.

One of the regular habitués of the Hotel cheerfully suggested that I sublease a room in the office suite he and his business partner rented nearby. When I went over to look at the room, only the business partner was there. He apparently had not been informed of the possibility that a tarot card reader might be moving in. It was an awkward afternoon.

After that, David and I scouted around various office buildings for the perfect location. We were pretty sure that we did not want to be in a strip shopping center, for two reasons.

First, we wanted to distance ourselves as much as possible from the typical "neon reader" set up, so no strip shopping center, no ratty house, no neon for us. (I realize that for some, the "neon reader" image will be perfect, but it's just not our style.)

Second, as we mentioned to clients and colleagues that we were looking for an office space, our clients gently suggested that we find a space where it would be difficult for someone to watch them go in through our door. Privacy is a high priority for many of our clients. (Indeed, private investigators and paparazzi are frequently lurking about in our parking lot!) The privacy-for-clients issue eliminated strip shopping centers and also knocked out the idea of officing with other practitioners in some sort of holistic center.

A private office in an office building seemed our best (and perhaps our only) choice.

One night, as I was driving home by myself in the wee hours of the morning after a party, something told me to take a turn down a street I normally don't frequent. This street is only about a mile from my house, but I had never paid it much attention. I came upon a small office building complex and jotted down the phone number. I called the next day, ran over and checked out several single offices and suites that were available.

It only took David and I about a day of deliberation to decide that this was the perfect spot for our office. The location was extremely easy to find, right off of a main highway, not far from downtown. It had plenty of parking, and the building was quite small.

The building was at least thirty years old and pretty dilapidated, but we thought that might actually be a plus.

A professional curandero once told me that he made a point of selecting office locations that weren't ever too nice, and he always made the interior interesting, but ratty. He believed his clients expected this and he never wanted to appear flashy. I think he believed that the clients would think him less spiritual if he appeared too preoccupied with ostentatious finery and too successful in the material world. He has a point! Folks in our business frequently become targets when we become successful.

My personal belief is that this reflects the discomfort society has always had with spiritual practitioners. They are not sure what to do with us! We don't fit in and we are not controllable. We seem safer to society in general if we seem to not care about the material world.

The "neon readers" know this, and that is why they will rent a small junky house or retail location to do readings in. If their space is in an old house, they may furnish the rooms to make it look like they actually live there and are reading for you in the front parlour, but they actually live elsewhere, in a very much nicer house.

When you are shopping for your office, think carefully through and balance ideas of your comfort and convenience, accessibility by your clients, not causing trouble where you might decide to office, and your clients' comfort and expectations. What I mean by not causing trouble goes back to not being too blatant about who you are and what your business is.

In my office building, there are two Baptist churches. The largest one takes up almost the entire main hallway in my building. I rarely do readings on Sundays, and see only two clients at the most on Wednesday evenings, the times when this church is very busy. My office is right around the corner from this church, but I'm pretty sure most of the congregation has no idea who I am and what I do. Sometimes I will go in on a Sunday just to prop open my door, putter around the office and listen to the fabulous live gospel music wafting down my hallway. Low profile is good!

Speaking of religion, I feel pretty strongly that professional readers need to be professional, and not announce religious preference or get on a soapbox about history, religion, etc. Do you really care about the religion of your accountant or dentist? We are service providers, not champions for The One Right Way To Live. Yes, we are dealing with spiritual matters as a course of our business, but anything that polarizes you and your clientele or office neighbours, anything that makes them uncomfortable, is just wrong.

The clients who come to you will be of every possible religious background and lifestyle persuasion. If you have some sort of persecution complex or are uncomfortable with people who live differently than you, you need to clean that mess up before you decide to become a professional reader!

Our location is extremely easy for clients to find, even clients who are from out of town and unfamiliar with our city. Our location also is innocuous and invisible.

When our clients mentioned that they didn't want to be seen coming to get readings from us, we paid attention to them. I would suggest that you do the same. Discretion of location is a prime consideration if you plan on having upscale or high profile clients. Someone who has a very visible standing in the community will not risk scandal or ridicule by being seen coming to you, no matter how good you are.

I know it's not fair! Many things are not fair. Get over it.

When it came time to select what sort of signage to have, I decided to have only my name and suite number on the door of my office. I am not even listed in the directory in the lobby of my building. I am very high profile on the internet, and I am high profile in my city (I do plenty of media-related projects and David and I are the go-to folks for metaphysical subjects for the local media, as we are always seen as extremely cooperative and a really fun interview), but I am very discreet in my office building. I am sure that this has warded off problems before they could begin. Familiarity breeds contempt. David and I are always extremely cordial and polite to the other tenants in our building, but we try very hard not to engage with them much.

Before we ever opened our office, we had an idea of how we wanted it to look and feel. We knew we would be spending a considerable amount of time there.

I wanted it to feel as much like home as possible, because I knew that if it didn't feel like that, I would end up avoiding going into work. I knew that I would love my office if it felt like an extension of my home, and I was still in love with the vintage fortune telling parlour concept.

We both knew that we didn't want it to look like a Gypsy shop, and we didn't want a Zen sort of look or a New Age look. We played with, and let go of, a high Art Deco look, like a Chanel boutique. (I still think that would be hilarious, and very pretty.) In the end, we decided that we wanted to be comfortable, we wanted our clients to have a unique experience when they came to visit us, and we didn't want our offices to look like anything else.

Because I am fascinated with and trained in hoodoo, and needed to store a large quantity of vintage jars full of various herbs and roots at the office, as well as carry a line of Lucky Mojo Curio Company products, we decided to make the front room reminiscent of New Orleans in the 1920s, all soft greens and cream. It's a beautiful room. When clients visit for the first time, they are stunned to walk in the door and feel like they are in another world.

David and I have individual offices, where we conduct our private sessions.

My office is all red and gold, full of fringe, tassels, funky antiques, and my extensive collection of vintage fortune teller photographs. It's a magical space!

David's office is very masculine and Edwardian. He wanted it to look as if Edward Gorey had designed it, and I do believe he succeeded.

It may seem to some that we put too much emphasis on surface appearances. (I can hear the distant chorus of voices saying "What does all this talk about interior decoration have to do with astrology and tarot card reading?")

You must remember that David and I both come from a professional art, design, and show business background. We are both acutely aware of the impact environment has on an individual. We were careful to design spaces to please ourselves first.

The fact that our clients find our environments so delightful is a plus. I believe that our clients receive extra value from us, both because they have to make a special journey to visit us, and because the environments we are in make them feel as if they are stepping out of the real world for a short time. Like an induction technique in hypnosis, stepping into our office plunges them into a different world and makes them more aware, clearer, more observant, and more detached about their own current life situations.

Talk to the Other Tenants

Before signing the lease, you might want to stop by your potential office during a business day and wander around. Pretend you are a client coming to see you.

How difficult is it to find your office? Where are the bathrooms?

During your wandering see if you can strike up some conversations with a few tenants and ask them how happy they are with their office. In Texas we have extremes of temperature, especially in the summertime. All of the tenants I spoke to before moving into our office informed me that the antiquated cooling system wasn't really sufficient during the dog days of summer. Knowing this, I was prepared to buy an auxiliary cooling system for our office, to keep it relatively comfortable in the summer.

Ask Questions of the Landlord

Renting an office means signing a lease. These leases are usually pretty standard, but before you sign that lease, ask the landlord a few questions:

How often is the building cleaned and maintained?

What is included in the lease? (Utilities are usually included, but ask!)

How difficult and expensive it is to run in a phone line? (This is only really a problem if you think you need to run in a line for a fax or a fast cable line for internet. Our office is so old and the building walls have been moved around so many times that running in a dedicated phone line is now prohibitively expensive.)

Will you have 24 hour access?

What kind of security is provided?

Smoke and Flame

Candles and incense are always a problem. Just be careful about this.

Your lease may prohibit burning any kind of candle. If that is the case, you may need to work with artificial candles to create the ambience you want.

David and I do burn candles, but we are extremely careful about how we use them. Two of my dearest friends and colleagues who are both ministers and run a local church in a nearby shopping center, had a tragic situation a few years back, where a simple tea light left burning on an altar started a blaze. They managed to rebuild, but it was a terrible situation, made more terrible because it could've easily been prevented.

Incense, also, can seem intrusive to the other occupants of your building. The smoke detectors in my building are heat sensitive, so incense will not set them off, thank God. Even so, if I'm using incense, I try to use it in the middle of the night when none of the other occupants are present.

Refurbish or Remodel?

Our building is dilapidated enough that the building manager doesn't mind our painting of our offices and installing elaborate window treatments and other decorative elements … so David built a gorgeous faux fireplace into his office!

Before you do anything like this, check with your landlord and make sure it will be okay. We have made it very clear to him that when we move, we will repaint the walls the basic white, repair any damage, and leave the suite in perfect, rentable condition.

References

In order to rent the office, you may be required to supply a recommendation from a previous office landlord. This could be a bit of a problem if this is your first office!

Be creative with this. If you know anyone who owns a commercial building, see if they will vouch for you. I had never rented an office prior to this. The year before, though, David and I had leased space during Halloween at a prominent local horror theme park to handle the fortune telling concession. The guy who managed the park loved us, because we created a very special attraction, and left the site nicer than we had found it when he leased it to us. I gave his contact information to my new landlord, and that was all it took.

Don't let small things like this get in your way; they are just details.

An Office Assistant

I have gone back-and-forth for many years over whether or not to have an assistant or secretary in the front room of my office, managing things while I do readings back in my reading room. When David and I were trying to figure out the schedule we wanted, we toyed with the idea of having someone in the front room to answer the phone, process credit cards, answer the door, make coffee or tea, and offer beverages and cookies to waiting clients.

We hired a wonderful gal to do this for a while, and one day while I was with a client I heard quite a commotion in the front room. I continued with my session. Afterwards I asked her what had happened. She said someone had knocked on the door and she had answered. A very obnoxious man had inserted himself into the office and demanded to see me. He began railing on about how evil any sort of fortune telling is, and thrust a bunch of religious tracts at her. He really wanted to disrupt my session with my client and speak to me. My lovely assistant Rebecca would not let him, marvellous girl that she is! Never assume that a Libra is a pushover. She was kind, gracious, and stubbornly not about to budge and let this horrible man interrupt me, God bless her!

I relate this story here to plant the idea in your head that it might be a fantastic idea to hire someone to manage the "front of the house" if you are planning on doing readings back-to-back. There is only so much you can handle at one time, and your responsibility to your clients is to give them your full attention when you are in a session with them.

When I got away from scheduling clients back-to-back, there simply was not enough for the secretary to do to justify the expense of hiring her. I currently see about three or four clients a day. I spread them out so I have time in between to answer my phone, deal with my emails and paperwork, and be fresh for each client. I still miss the lovely Rebecca, and I make it a point to keep my front door securely locked when I am in a session with a client.

Office Essentials

Here are the basics you'll need to get started in your private office:
- A table where you do the readings
- A very comfortable chair for you
- Between 2 and 4 chairs for clients
- Sufficient lighting
- A computer and a printer
- A telephone
- A website and a professional email address
- Quality business cards

These are things you might want to add to make life a little nicer:
- A microwave
- A small refrigerator
- A coffee maker and an electric tea kettle
- Coffee mugs, tea cups, water glasses, and cutlery (chinaware, not styrofoam!)
- A small cupboard for kitchen supplies
- Auxiliary air conditioning
- Auxiliary small heaters
- Comfortable sofa and chairs for waiting clients
- Books and magazines for waiting clients
- A CD player
- A tiny TV, hooked up to play DVDs
- An assortment of DVDs for young children

The basics need no further explanation, but let me explain about a few of the seeming luxuries.

The microwave is obvious: If we are stuck at the office during a meal time, we always have choices in our small refrigerator that could be heated up and eaten.

I have already explained about the dicey heating and air conditioning in our old building. There have been many summers where it was so swelteringly hot, I literally could not have read for clients at all without my extra air-conditioning.

The niceties for waiting clients are also obvious, and, of course, they should harmonize with the rest of your office decor.

The tiny television and the DVDs for children are a real lifesaver if a client shows up with a small child. This doesn't happen very often, but when it does, it can be a real disaster. Nobody can tend a child and get a reading at the same time. I guarantee you that your client's sleeping toddler will suddenly pop wide awake the instant the client crosses the threshold into your office. (It's like magic!)

If you have a tiny TV and a stash of children's videos, you are saved. Prop the child up in front of the television in your front room, where you can keep an eye on them. The little one will be glassy eyed, hypnotized by the television before you know it, and the reading can commence.

Even if you have a policy of allowing no children in your office, you will occasionally have clients who run into a sudden no-nanny, no-babysitter situation. Be prepared.

Do You Really Need an Office?

If all of this sounds too complicated and expensive, you are probably thinking that the best idea is just to see clients in your home, but really, if you are truly serious about a professional, full-time career as a reader, it will probably be necessary at some point to open an actual office. Even if you are determined to only read over the phone or Skype, there will be clients in your community who will want a private reading from you.

Is it is possible to see clients in your home?

Yes.

Is seeing clients in your home ideal?

No, there are obviously some problems with this.

You may live in a community that has laws about home-based businesses. (I have heard about situations where the laws would make phone reading in your home illegal! Seriously, how would they ever even know you were doing that?) Even if you are allowed to read in your home, there may be laws having to do with signage and potentially too much traffic in the neighbourhood. Please be aware of the legal rules in your area, and abide by them.

A bigger problem than zoning or legal issues is the issue of safety. If you decide to read in your home, you MUST not be there alone. You will have to hire (or live with) someone to be a presence, even if they have no other duties. If you are female, hire a male to do this. Even if all he does is answer the door and bring coffee as you begin your session, the silent message is clear … you are watched and protected. I get a bit hysterical at the idea of strangers in my home (fourth house Scorpio), so I could never office out of my house.

A local reader who read at a bar was hassled by the abusive ex-boyfriend of a client she had read for. The client had dumped the guy, and he blamed the reader. He showed up at the bar to abuse and intimidate the reader and was escorted away by the bouncer. What if she read from her home and not at that bar? What would have happened when Crazy Dude showed up on her doorstep? I shudder to think!

Remember, if you hire someone to be your wrangler at your home during your work hours, what will happen during off-hours when they aren't around? Do you have a husband or boyfriend in attendance as a full-time wrangler and bouncer?

If you have an office away from your home, this won't be an issue because you won't be there. Also, people will tend to be more careful about behaviour in a professional setting. If you office in a professional office area, there will be many other people around (witnesses!), and it will slow down the likelihood of an incident.

Remember my story about Rebecca and the Jesus Dude who wanted to interrupt my session? I am pretty sure he found me on the internet and decided his mission was to shut me down. What if he had shown up at my house? I probably would have had to call the police. Think of all of the time and aggravation that would have caused! I am sure the police would have been very sympathetic towards the poor tarot card reader. (Yes, I meant that sarcastically.)

Many of my colleagues will not agree with me on my views of reading out of the home, as the home reading parlour is a long and respected tradition in our field. They may say that they choose clients carefully and therefore have no problems.

Your problems may not be with a client! Your problem could be with a random nutjob like the Jesus Dude or the Rejected Abusive Boyfriend.

Is it really worth the risk?

Can You Afford an Office?

If you think you cannot afford office space, you probably haven't actually looked very hard. Every city has small single-office rooms to rent. Some even have rent-by-the-hour conference rooms in suites that include a receptionist and a mailing address! You price your fee to include the cost of this space.

Alternatively, you could share a small office space with another practitioner and take turns wrangling for each other.

You could also look into renting space at a local holistic or spiritual center; they frequently have offices to rent for metaphysical practitioners and wellness professionals.

The Rural Reader's Office Possibilities

If you live in an area that is extremely rural, remote, or unsophisticated, you may have to do a little PR for yourself before renting an office or finding a venue to read from. You will have to become known and be seen as fun, amusing, and harmless. Here's how to do it:

Read regularly for friends at a local (non-corporate chain) bar or restaurant. Palmistry or playing-card readings are perfect for this. Leave the tarot cards at home; those classic images on tarot cards may be just too much for some folks. Have uproarious fun at your table reading for your buddies. Look happy and cute, not weird and spooky.

I promise you, if you start reading (especially reading palms!) in a place like this during a busy time, everyone in the place will want you to come to their table and read for them. Do a few readings (leave them wanting more), make the readings awesome and hilarious, don't ask for a fee (never, unless the management has okayed this!), and just tell everyone that you are looking for a place to office out of. In a small town, everyone knows everyone, and eventually someone will think of a place for you, or can call someone for you. Don't cold-call an office landlord; have someone call for you who has seen your marvellous work.

This is what will happen next: The manager at the restaurant will notice what a stir you make every time you are there reading for your pals, and may ask you to be there regularly. don't expect the manager to actually hire you; they won't usually be able to do that. The manager may suggest everything from you paying a set fee to be there (don't do it!), to giving the House a percentage of your takings for each evening (that is fair), to please just be here to create an attraction and keep whatever money you make (fantastic!).

You might have to cheerfully decline the manager's first offer or idea about this, which will usually include you paying him to be there; do not act all offended and get pissy, just explain that you are SO flattered, but really can't afford that right now. Be kind and friendly and keep showing up with friends and creating a sensation. Eventually, he will come up with a better plan.

Be at that location regularly, show up when expected, be amazing and fun, and develop friendships with the Regulars. Eventually, someone will come up with an arrangement that will work out as an office space for you.

I know that most truly rural readers rely primarily (or only) on phone readings, as there just won't be enough population to justify opening an office; I still think it is sort of insane to do readings out of your home.

My point is just to be aware and be careful. Not everyone thinks readers are awesome, and there are plenty of crazy folks out there.

An Interview with Marin Graves,
An Office Reader

Marin Graves is the proprietor of one of the most charming tarot boutiques in America, The Parlour in Grass Valley, California. Her space is decorated in Victorian style and located in a picturesque little Gold Rush town in the Sierra Mountain foothills. She supplements her walk-in trade with telephone readings and spiritual rootwork for internet clients.

Val: Tell us about The Parlour and why you created it.

Marin: I started in 2006, working out of an office space I shared with a therapeutic hypnotist. In 2007, when the business was on a firm footing, I created The Psychic Tarot Parlour in Nevada City. In 2011, I moved to a new space in Grass Valley. I live between Grass Valley and Nevada City, so I can locate in either direction.

Nevada City is a more eclectic town, and it gave me confidence to start out there. There were two other readers, one calling herself a Psychic Reader and one calling herself a Spiritual Counsellor. What I did that was different, based on a spiritual vision I had, was to create a Victorian space to fit the historic surroundings. The Gold Rush area is a tourist destination year 'round. In the summers there is camping, fishing, gold panning, and gold mine tours, and in winter the emphasis is on Victorian Christmas and boutique shopping. Other psychics nearby had never been attentive to the decor, so I wanted my space to be like someone was stepping back in time a little bit.

Val: In Nevada City your office was The Psychic Tarot Parlour, but when you moved to Grass Valley, your name changed. You lost the "Psychic Tarot" and are now The Parlour.

Marin: The move and the name-change were not pre-planned. They came about fortuitously. I take my kids down the same route every day and I passed this historic building in Grass Valley every day and I always thought this corner space was the cutest space. One day I was driving by with my husband and I told him how much I liked it, and he said, "Why don't you just pull over and see what they want for it?" It was in my price range, it had parking, and the owner paid all the utilities, so by that night I had already mentally redecorated it, and the next day I called them and said, "Okay I'm doing it."

Zoning turned out to be the biggest hurdle. Every city or county has zoning ordinances, and Grass Valley, unlike Nevada City, allows no tattoo artists, no fortune tellers, no palm readers, and no card readers. I was advised that the name "Psychic" could be reported to the the police and I might have to close my business. But at the same time, I felt like I was getting more into the counselling aspects of reading and I was okay letting go of the word "Psychic."

Val: So how have things turned out in the new location, with the tighter zoning?

Marin: I have never had a complaint or investigation. For the first three months, I kept my curtains down, but now I leave one central curtain open, and you can see the table, crystal ball, two chairs, Victorian pictures, and the crystal chandelier. I would like to have a larger sign, but we need to have sign permits, and that would draw attention,

I have lived in this town over 25 years and feel I am enough of a member of this community to address any concerns if they did come up. I have two very young kids and I didn't want them being mocked in school, but now I'm known as "the psychic football mom." When people find out who I am, they say, "Oh, that's *your* space? Oh, that's so *cute!*" So it's not a stigma. I feel very well received.

Val: The interior decoration is so beautiful.

Marin: Thank you. The furniture and decor was obtained locally and from Craigslist. Everything's antique, bought piece by piece. I did the painting myself. The walls are ivory, rag-rolled with gold. I have a gold ceiling, and the 78 cards of the extra large Rider Waite Tarot border the ceiling moulding. The pictures on the walls I got by making Google image searches for "crystal ball" and "psychic reader." I printed them out and framed them.

I have a set of card racks spray-painted gold, containing 30 tarot decks. I used to allow clients to select their deck, but that invited an unpaid half an hour conversation about how exciting it was to choose their deck, so I moved the rack of decks behind me. Now I choose the deck, but if they are very attracted to a certain deck and say, "Oh, I love that deck," then I can just choose that deck. I have about 80 decks now. I rotate them through the racks.

In the North corner of the room, which provides grounding (that's from my Wicca tradition), is my working altar for rootwork clients. It is out of the field of vision of sitting clients. They see a display of herbs, the cards in their racks, and a mirror, but the burning candles and the altar are to their backs, so they are not distracted by the lights of the candles.

Val: How does your walk-in trade compare to scheduled in-person or phone readings?

Marin: Walk-ins are about 10% of my business, but I only have one day for walk-ins, Friday. Pre-scheduled in-person readings account for 20%, pre-scheduled phone readings through the Association of Independent Readers and Rootworkers are 30%, and readings via the psychic lines are 40%. My biggest days are Friday, Saturday, and Sunday, plus Monday on the longer, extended holiday weekends.

Val: How do you advertise The Parlour?.

Marin: My advertising is 90% word of mouth. I have never had a Yellow Pages ad, but I put up business cards on local community cork boards in coffee shops and grocery stores. I pay $150.00 for an ad in a local yearly listing of psychics, holistic wellness bodyworkers, and metaphysical workers. I get very little clientele from that — I may get only three people per year from that — but it gives me legitimacy in the community and they offer other perks. I pay $100.00 per year for my web site directory listing in AIRR. As I said, this brings in 30% of my income, but it has not resulted in any local in-person readings, due to my rural location.

Val: One last question: What do you like the most about reading in an office?

Marin: One of the nicest things about having my Parlour is that it feels like sacred space. I don't have to worry about having the kids' clutter in the dining room. Even my private space at home does not have that feeling. I use this space for meditation and prayer.

Nuts

On a dark and stormy night, the final client of the day arrives at my office.

A red-faced woman enters the room in a rather fun holiday-themed sweater.

We begin her reading and I lay out the cards. Before I'm able to speak, she blurts out, "Is there anything in those cards about the dentists? You know, the dentists! They are all trying to file down my teeth!"

I take a breath, too shocked to laugh; I decide to soldier on with the reading.

She poses yet another question, this time really aggravated: "What do you see about my husband, the psychiatrist? He's invited someone to our house, he says it's just a friend, I think it's a colleague who is coming to observe me, so he can have me committed! They've been planning it for years!"

I realize I still have another 40 minutes with this woman.

To change the subject, I segue into commenting on details in her astrological chart. Once again, she begins to rant: "I know those people that killed Marilyn and the Kennedys are after me! It's because I know too much. That's why my children don't want to be around me, they'd be in danger, too!"

They have a saying in the circus, about ærial performers, that there are only two types, those who have fallen, and those who are going to fall. If you read much for the public at all, you will have one of these clients and you must handle the situation gracefully.

You have to realize that this person's problem is way beyond your abilities, and a tarot reading is not what is needed.

I will usually gently tell these clients, "Something has thrown your chemistry off, and I can't read for you again until you get your chemistry stabilized." (And a big thank-you to my teacher Catherine Yronwode, who originally suggested saying something like this in just this sort of situation.)

Reading at Psychic Fairs

Psychic fairs fall into three categories: Local, Mid-Size, and Exposition-Size. Each of these types of venues has its own culture and carries with it a certain set of expectations with respect to how readers are integrated into the event. In addition, non-psychic fairs often hire readers, as do corporate trade show events.

The Small, Local Event

The first category, the small, local fair, includes events that are connected with a bookstore, occult shop, or metaphysical center. There may be a few vendors, or just one vendor (the shop or center mounting the show), who will typically invite all of the local readers to participate.

These fairs can be fun and have a very friendly feel to them because they are so small. Unless the bookstore, occult shop, or metaphysical center knows how to market the fair, or the event has been going on for a very long time and is well known in the local area, attendance at these fairs can be really spotty.

Usually, you will pay a small fee for table space at the fair. You will set your own price; bring your own props, table decor, and signage; and manage your own appointment times. One positive aspect of managing your own space at such a fair is that you will be allowed to hand out your business cards and other literature.

A day at one of these fairs is plenty of fun, but if your goal is to have a really financially successful day, or to cultivate new clients for your private practice, you may be disappointed. You could have made more money by booking full-length sessions at your office.

On the positive side, however, if you are very new to this work, have not yet set up a private office, and want to test the waters by reading at the local store or center first, then participating in their event allows you to show yourself off to the person who arranges for readers there. In other words, you may get an offer to work at the shop or center.

The Mid-Size Psychic Fair

The second kind of psychic fair will be larger, with from 30 to 100 readers. These sorts of fairs are usually held in a hotel ballroom or larger event space.

Many of these fairs handle all of the money and pay the readers at the conclusion of the fair or in the week following. You do not have to pay for your table space at this sort of fair because the organizers make money by taking a percentage of each reading that you do.

Frequently, the managers of mid-sized psychic fairs organize the reading schedules and allotted reading times for each reader, usually by collecting the money and giving the clients a chit or ticket to redeem for their readings. The fair management decides the length of the readings and the price. You will not be allowed to deviate from the allotted reading time, because running overtime with a client will throw everybody else off too.

These fairs are not so big that you lose the very warm, pleasant feeling of the smaller fairs, but you may run into more issues with jealousy and unpleasant people.

My experience has been that the mid-size fairs reflect the people who own and run them, and if the fair is run by somebody who is fun, happy, temperate, and charming, the experience of being at that fair for the day will be the same.

The Large Psychic Expo

The third kind of fair is the enormous expo that appears, sometimes seasonally, in most large cities. These events are huge, attracting thousands of people. They usually will run over at least two, and sometimes three days. They are almost never advertised as a psychic fair, but usually as a Holistic Expo, Healing Expo, Body-Mind-Spirit Expo, or something like that. You will find many psychics there, and also healers, visionaries, and folks selling all sorts of alternative, therapeutic, and healing products. There will be food vendors in attendance and there may be times set aside for on-stage music as well. These events may be held in convention centers, fairgrounds, or other large venues.

At one of these body, mind, and spirit expos, you will purchase your own booth space. This can be pretty expensive, as the booths usually start in the hundreds of dollars. You need to be prepared by having appropriate and attractive signage for your booth, cool looking decorative stuff for your booth, plenty of handouts (business cards and brochures), and something that will make people stop and pay attention.

These expos are essentially enormous trade shows, so the guests step in and are overwhelmed by all of the offerings, the sights, sounds, and smells. If you can find a way to stand out and be different, to offer something you can do at a relatively low price and quickly, you will be a success. Consider an unusual divination technique, not the usual tarot.

As with any trade show, working one of these events is a real grind. It's a great idea to organize yourself beforehand and bring with you water, food, and possibly a very comfortable chair. Expos can really wear you out!

An expo or really large psychic fair is another situation where using a wrangler is a very good idea. Since you are responsible for setting fees and managing the collection of money, it's great to have someone who can do that and have conversations with potential clients while you are in the middle of a private reading. Otherwise, I promise you, you will have a pile of people interrupting you to ask you questions, just as you begin a private session!

Be sure to advertise your upcoming presence at the expo on your website and blog, and at all of your online social networking sites. Ask if the expo will send you some advance publicity material. If they do, then staple a notice with your booth number to each ad sheet and hand the ad sheets out to your office clients during the month leading up to the expo. The expo managers will be doing a lot of publicity for the event, of course, but you want to help them, and to spread the word among your regular clients that you will be there.

Going on the Expo Circuit

If you decide to work at psychic fairs or expos that are out of town, you will need to be careful about the extra expenses incurred.

Check around and see if other readers are coming in from out of town, and if there is some kind of a discount available at a local hotel or maybe at the hotel where the expo is being held. Find out how many people are reading tarot, and be prepared to offer something different.

Calculate in the cost of gas, possibly airfare, and meal expenses on top of the cost of your booth, to see if it is even possible for you to make more money at the expo than you would by seeing private clients in your office.

Always post notices well in advance of these events on your web site, blog, or social networking sites, announcing when and where the expo is, with your booth number.

Themed (Non-Psychic) Fairs

Themed fairs include events such as Renaissance fairs, Dickens fairs, historical re-enactments, seasonal public fairs, music festivals, Halloween parks, and civic fetes.

Renaissance fairs are generally large and well-established outdoor events. Fortunetellers are common and welcomed, but there may be a long waiting list to even be considered for a spot, because regular readers at Ren fairs keep their spots for years. Dickens fairs and Victorian Christmases are much like Ren fairs, but they are held in the cooler months, so they are often located indoors. If you like the fair circuit, you can book yourself almost year 'round with Ren fairs, Dickens fairs, and Victorian Christmas venues. These fairs have a circuit (like the old vaudeville days!), so if you can get in, and find you like these venues, you can create a tour for yourself and do a series of fairs every year.

Historically-themed events usually have strict guidelines about presentation: Your wardrobe and equipment must be as accurate as possible. Meeting these requirements can be fun if you enjoy costuming and the use of vintage divination tools. In addition, if you are a performer, you'll get the opportunity to develop your own historically-based character.

Outdoor fairs bring their own challenges and joys. First, look over the layout: Getting stuck next to a noisy Main Stage (or worse, next to three rows of porta-potties) can ruin your experience. Second, consider the weather: In some areas, summer heat and humidity are unbearable, and mosquitoes are a problem. Third, strategize your endurance: Costumes which were fun for the first weekend will eventually become oppressive and stinky. You will need props that are impervious to breakage and fabrics that can be easily cleaned.

Do you actually know how to set up that tent you just rented for the run of the fair?
What will you do if you get to your space and the ground is all flooded and swampy?
If it rains the whole weekend, how will you stay dry and in a good humour?
How will you pack up quickly and get yourself to safety if there is a sudden tornado?
How will you take bathroom breaks without leaving your tent unattended?
When working an outdoor event, plan for anything to happen, because it will!

Then there's the money angle: Most themed fairs charge a flat fee for your space for the run of the fair. A few also want a percentage of your gross, and you must keep records of total sales, and figure that in. Pricing your readings is up to you. Keep the readings short and the price low. You want to be doing readings all day and you don't need any price resistance. Visit a few fairs in your area and investigate the pricing structure of the readers.

If you have paid $500.00 to be a vendor, and you plan to charge $10.00 for ten minute readings, then, you can reasonably expect to do three readings an hour. Some will say this is a ridiculously low expectation, but in my experience, it is very rare to do readings back-to-back all day. Most events like these have their heaviest attendance between noon and 6:00 pm. Thirty dollars an hour times six hours is $180.00 per day. Three days of that is $540.00! And that is if the event isn't rained out or poorly attended.

One way to increase your income is to have more than one reader in your tent, but even then, you have to like what you are doing, because a fair is always a financial gamble. You have the overhead of the rental fee to cover before you ever see a penny of profit, and a rainy weekend with poor attendance can easily wipe out any potential profit.

Working at a fair can make you a better reader by getting you out there reading for all sorts of folks. If you are starting your career, it will help you promote your name. If you like costuming and character acting, it is great fun. But it is very rarely a financial triumph.

Corporate Events

Corporate events are almost always booked through an entertainment agent. If you decide to work these types of events, you must aim your marketing towards agents. Your pricing should be in line with other local entertainers' fees, so do your research.

At a corporate event, you are a hired entertainer. Your goal is to get to as many guests as possible and delight them with your amazing skills. The problem with this goal is that the usual set-up of fortuneteller-behind-a-table, reading one-guest-at-a-time really doesn't allow you to read for very many people.

David and I will frequently stand behind our tables to read cards at a large corporate party (no chairs for guests or reader!), or we will wear cigarette-girl style trays that give us a surface to lay out a single card as we do strolling readings. Both of these techniques speed the reading process up immeasurably. If the guests do not sit, they do not get comfortable and you can send them on their way after the short reading. Strolling with a tray keeps you in charge of how long the reading is for each guest. However, even if there are two of you doing three-minute readings, you will get to only forty guests per hour. If you are performing at a large event you will disappoint many folks by not having time to read for them.

I would like to suggest a couple of great books that address this issue and solve it beautifully. "Gypsies Go Roving" and "The Book Of Roving," by Sheila Lyon and Mark Sherman, will teach you how to read for large crowds of people and keep them very happy by getting them actively involved in the readings.

The only disagreement I have with Sheila and Mark's approach is that they recommend that the reader not sit down in a tent or behind a table. I, on the other hand, LOVE it when I have a fabulous tent or fortuneteller area at an event! David and I specialize in amazing costuming, and I like being a big part of the scenery at a party. I am only 5' 3" tall , so I can easily get lost in a crowd of tall people unless I am elevated, have on a big headdress, have a backdrop, or have a tent to stand in.

Trade Shows

Trade shows are booked like corporate events, through entertainment agents, but they are more interesting and tough because you are not just hired as an entertainer.

If you are in a trade show booth, you are representing the company that has bought the booth. Everything you do must be flawless, and your job is to create a memorable and happy experience for everyone who sets foot in that booth.

The folks working the booth will be trying to network with the trade show attendees. The reason they will have hired you is as an attraction to draw people into the booth.

Elevate the surface you are reading on. Put a large box on your table under your tablecloth and stand up so people can see you. Wear your brightest and most fun costume. Smile and be warm and charming. Do quick and positive readings.

Do not get in the way of sales staff in the booth talking to potential clients. If your client asks you to season your readings with a little bit of "I see you making a very wise decision to use YXZ Company for all of your Widget needs," don't get pissy, just have fun with it.

If you can get lots of laughter and joking going in your booth from your readings, that will attract people. I usually will have people who are hosting other booths trying to hire me for the next trade show by the time I finish for the day, and that is very satisfying!

An Interview with Cheryl Andrea McMillan, Owner of the Dallas Psychic Fair

The Dallas Psychic Fair is a mid-size fair held monthly in a hotel ballroom in Dallas, TX. In addition to readers, the fair includes vendors and healers in a variety of traditions.

Val: You are a well known local intuitive with a private practice, and you have successfully stepped into owning and running the Dallas Psychic Fair, among other big projects! How did you get to this point? What led you to it?

Cheryl: My transition to being an intuitive reader was kind of funny. I'm a massage therapist and I have yoga instructor certification. That was how I made my way out of the corporate world into my own practice. I was doing something that I believed was not too offensive to people, massage and yoga.

I was working with a massage client one time, and when I put my hand on the woman's shoulders, I sort of spontaneously said, "Oh, you've been planting flowers." She stiffened and said, "Yes, how did you know that?" I responded with, "Well, you know, these muscles up here are…" and I hear immediately God say to me, "Never invalidate that which you are!"

And so out of my mouth comes, "Well, actually, oftentimes when I place my hands on someone I receive information." Of course, then she wants to test it, so she says, "What colour were they?" And I fall for it. I say, "They were pink and yellow and orange!" She got very stiff. She didn't say another word to me for the rest of the session. She got up, she walked out, and I have never seen her again, but she profoundly changed how I experience my own authenticity. If I could find that woman (and I have tried!) I would tell her, "Thank you!"

Val: Why did you decide to do the massage and yoga work?

Cheryl: I worked helping to run and grow a company, at the same time secretly putting myself through massage school, so I would never have to put my children in day care.

It was mindfully done. I knew I didn't want to be a single mom and work forty-plus hours a week, and have my son in daycare after school all those extra hours. And I didn't really ever want to work for someone else. So I made the decision at twenty five, and I just did it. By the time I was twenty seven, I was self-employed and had my first business.

But, when I stepped away from my real job, I literally had no clients! And, at the same time, my ex-husband decided to stop paying child support! So, I'm twenty five. I have a young child. I have animals. I have bills to pay and no visible way to pay them. I sat in my apartment for a whole day, crying and smoking cigarettes.

An inner voice kept saying "You wouldn't have even made it through massage school if you weren't right where you are supposed to be."

Truly, the divine order of how all of that happened was amazing! The funding to do it, the year-long process, the experience itself!

"You wouldn't be here if you weren't on the right path."

That thought kept coming up over and over and over again. I'm crying and smoking and trying to figure out what I'm going to do. I've procrastinated about going down to the mailbox, afraid of all the bills I'm going to find there. I was in total fear.

Finally, that evening I got my nerves together and went down to the mailbox. I opened it up, and with all the bills was a letter from a dentist I hadn't seen in years, with a $400.00 refund check from some dental work I had apparently overpaid years before! Now, who does that? Those sorts of things don't happen!

That was a pivotal moment for me to learn to never doubt that if we show up and say yes, the rest of it is details. I just have to show up and say yes! That was one of the most magical experiences of my life.

Also, to make that transition, I determined that if I looked at the fact that I needed $2,500.00 a month to pay bills, I was going to be petrified, because I had associated fearful memories of what a dollar amount meant. So, I changed the way I looked at things and instead calculated it by how many massages I needed to do a month to meet my bills.

If I figured all I needed was to do thirty massages a month, well, that's only one per day! So, if on certain days I had three bookings and on other days I had none, I could have a sense of peace. I realized it was an ebb and flow, and I could more easily get over ideas and mental conditioning I had of scarcity, lack, and limitation around money. I reframed the way I told myself my personal story about money. Of course, you know the end of that! All of these people started showing up, all of these clients, because I had cleared the space for that.

Val: How did you go from massage therapist and yoga teacher to intuitive reader?

Cheryl: I was a closet reader for many years! I was so empathic that I was very concerned that calling myself a psychic and doing readings in the Bible Belt would be really offensive to other people's beliefs. I didn't like how that felt. I wasn't strong enough at the time to do that. I could work on people's bodies, and I understood the mind-body connection very well.

Finally, it got to the point where I saw those connections so well that I couldn't refrain from saying things like, "You know, this is about betrayal," or "Gosh, you're not feeling very supported in life right now are you?" in the middle of the massage! Those things kept happening! And people were coming to me and wanting readings without calling it a "reading." I just kept charging the same rate that I had charged for massage or yoga, and gradually the ratio of sessions that were "readings" far outweighed the others. So, I thought, "Well, I'm already doing it; I might as well claim it!" Then, it was a few years after that when the opportunity for the fair came around. Before the fair, I had been doing readings professionally for about 11 years.

Val: What made you decide to take on owning and running the Fair?

Cheryl: I didn't, God did! And that's a true story. Another example of showing up and saying yes!

Four years ago, I decided to refocus. I was in an uncomfortable marriage, and I decided to focus on myself and figure out what my purpose was. As I was thinking about this, I heard, "You better call the Dallas Psychic Fair because your time is running out."

I thought, I'm in private practice, what on earth do you want me to call the Fair for?

After some hemming and hawing, I called Rita and Barbara, the founders of the fair. I went and tested to be a reader at the fair. The third month I was reading at the fair, they handed us all postcards announcing that they were looking for someone to take over the fair. I knew immediately I was supposed to do this, and ran over and told them.

It actually never occurred to me that I would have to come up with money to buy this business. They interviewed a handful of people, and then decided that I should be the one to take over the fair. So I went and found investors. The universe made all of the money show up just in time, in sixty days.

Val: And you have done an incredible job of taking this marvellous fair and making it so much better! I am so proud of you! The fair is such a happy place.

Cheryl: Thank you! We've worked diligently to streamline everything. There are 40 readers now. There were only 25 when I took it over, so we have grown. We have big plans! I want to expand this successful model to other cities.

Val: What have you learned in taking on the fair?

Cheryl: One of the main things I learned that was really surprising to me, is that the readers are not interested in a unified cohesive collaborative group. I thought they would be!

Val: That surprises me! I would think they would be.

Cheryl: They really are more interested in what I can do for them. The model is set up that way, actually. We promote, we market, and we take a cut of their charges for doing that work. So in essence, yes, they are kind of coming into it where I do all the work. It's very lopsided. They just show up. Show up and read.

Val: Originally, wasn't a psychic fair set up sort of like a showcase? You would do these little readings as a taste for people who might want to become your client and get full sessions at another time.

Cheryl: That's right, the model was set up that way, where they are looking out only for themselves. But what I really was surprised about was how many of them really know nothing about business. They may be readers, but they know nothing about business. They know nothing about marketing themselves; they know nothing about the amount of work it takes to run a business, the amount of work it takes to get them out there!
I have policies and procedures for them all to sign now, and that's a very big deal. I found I needed them to be clear on what their job and their role was, and I wanted them to be clear on what my job and role was, what I would provide and what I was doing for them. I needed them to understand that it was give-and-take. I've learned about my ability to adapt. I've learned to stretch myself farther than I ever thought I could!

Val: What are your goals for the fair?

Cheryl: I want to take this very successful model — we are going into our twenty-ninth year of business — and grow it. I have watched about 15 different fairs come and go over the past 4 or 5 years. They start out and they don't make it. There are several reasons why they don't make it. And I think I understand what they are! So, without giving away the secret sauce, I realize that I have a model that works and my plan is to license it into other cities.

It's not about my ego. It's about having me share a model that works, so other communities can have a fair also. I'm looking for small fairs that are struggling or folks in the metaphysical community who love the idea of a fair but have no idea where to start to create one. I'm creating a template with everything someone would need to create a wildly successful fair in their community. I'm working on how to define that this year; that is my project.

Val: Well, I know you also have another project — you have started your own psychic phone line! Psychic Youniverse!

Cheryl: Last August, I suddenly had a whole day free because someone I was going to train called in sick. I was wondering what to do with my free day, when I heard that voice say, "Take a look at the phone lines again!"

I had all of these readers. Why not give them an opportunity to make some money outside of the fair, at home, the rest of the month? So I started Psychic Youniverse,

Val: What does somebody coming in as a reader need to know about what you might be looking for in a fair reader?

Cheryl: The first thing I'm looking for is if they can show up and be really present. Being present is incredibly important! Not, "Oh my God, my husband is driving me crazy; the kids are out of control, my life is full of drama!" They need to be able to be truly present in the middle of the chaos of the fair, with so many people around them — and not everybody can do that. Some people can't do it, some people don't want to do it and some people are just too empathic to put themselves through that. They can't handle an environment with that much energy.

I look for how much accurate and truly valuable information can they give in a very short period of time. They have to be confident, clear, and the reading jam-packed with information, not asking a bunch of questions of the client trying to figure it out.

Also I need to know that any prospective reader can stop the reading in fifteen minutes and not keep going and going and going! This is a sample reading, and it doesn't do you any good to give them too long of a reading. The idea is to give them a taste that will cause them then to buy a private session from you!

I'm also listening to their wording. I need them to be non-offensive, non-religious, and take their responsibility seriously. I want them to be mindful and respectful of the client.

I am looking for things like eye contact. I am looking for love and compassion. I can't have anybody at the fair who isn't all of these things.

One thing that sets us apart from other fairs is that we are highly discriminating about our readers. Most fairs will take just anybody, we will not. I have a vision and the readers can either rise up to that or they don't belong with us.

My intention is very clear about my three businesses. I know exactly what I want to do. I know exactly what I want them to be, how I want them to be streamlined, and I know exactly the kind of people I will need to put into key positions to grow those businesses the way I want to, so I can go create more stuff. I've always been a visionary.

Val: Cheryl, you are a treasure! Thank you for making time for this interview, busy lady!

Wise Guys

Some time last year, David was reading at the hotel.

A group of folks showed up who appeared to be business associates, and the Leader of the group wanted his cards read. Now, these guys were some pretty tough characters — let's just say easily interchangeable with the cast of "The Sopranos" — and David decided that their "business" was probably best not discussed in a public place.

The Leader's reading was interesting, and he insisted that everyone in the group get a reading.

So, one by one, David read for all of them, becoming more convinced with every reading that these guys were gangsters. Every time the cards mentioned a "Boss" everyone said that was "The Father" or "His Father," pointing at the Leader.

David was very nervous.

Just when he thought the ordeal was over, the Leader returned and wanted to ask a further question about his work. "I'm having difficulty with a certain person. I wanna know what this guy is gonna do, and how I can fix it."

David laid out the cards again. The Justice card was very prominent, and he realized it had been prominent in every single reading, for the entire group.

David threw caution to the winds and blurted out, "You know, the Justice card has come up in every single reading, for each of you guys. I feel like I'm reading for the Justice Department!"

The group cheered like someone had hit a jackpot. The Leader guy flashed a federal badge and hollered "Bingo! We are the number one fraud investigation team for the Treasury Department!"

David has never been so relieved.

ZOLEE
TELLS YOUR
PAST, PRESENT & FUTURE

Reading by Telephone

I have to admit that my least favourite way of doing readings is over the telephone. I have always given my clients successful readings by phone, but the readings are just not as much fun for me as reading face-to-face. However, for those who enjoy the work, doing phone readings does have certain obvious advantages over working in-person.

First, you are not spending any money on transportation to get to work, or spending any money on the overhead of a physical office. You do not have to look good or smell good, your house could be a disaster, and you are still at work and making money!

Second, it is a distraction-free way of reading: If you have your environment under control and peaceful, all you have to deal with is the voice on the other end of the phone and whatever divinatory tools you use. Obviously, a job where the biggest problem is dealing with emotional clients and laryngitis is a really great job. You, and you alone, are in charge of your schedule, your breaks, and the environment of your work, so there is a great deal of control.

Psychic Phone Line Basics

The easiest way to begin reading by phone is to sign up with an existing service or start your own solo phone practice. But first, you need to understand how these systems work.

When the psychic line business first started, the companies used 900-number lines and the per-minute charges were billed to the clients' phone bills. These Miss Cleo-type psychic lines generally set one per-minute fee for all clients and their readers made a tiny fraction of the fee that was charged to the client. Below minimum wage! Fantastic.

Due to the exposure of bad business practices in the 900-number lines (including scripts distributed to readers to teach them how to keep clients on the phone and racking up per-minute fees), the psychic line industry gradually shifted over to the use of 800-number lines.

These are toll-free lines, and the client's payment-clock only starts ticking when a reader picks up the phone and the conversation begins. The reader is an independent contractor, and the owner of the line charges a "connection fee" for putting the client together with the reader. You are only paid for the number of minutes the client is actually on the phone with you.

Some 800-number companies bill clients via credit card; other use third-party billing through the client's phone service. Each method has advantages and disadvantages.

Credit card billing requires pre-authorization, which is set for a pre-established maximum call time. If the authorization is for $240.00 or more (a 1-hour call at $4.00 per minute) many calls will fail the authorization process. Also, you cannot exceed the call-time (you will hear a warning; then the call cuts off). If the session is going well, you must ask the client to call back.

Third party billing sounds better in theory, because the call-time is completely open-ended and the charge is added to the client's phone bill, but in actual practice, there are more charge-backs with this system, as clients falsely claim, "I didn't know I was being charged."

Phone reading leaves you with little or no control over who your clients are, especially if you work through a phone service. If you are nervous about potentially having to read for crazy people, remember that you can always say a little prayer to set a powerful intention. I set an intention for every day of my work. I ask that it feel a certain way to me (calm, happy, fun, interesting), and that way I really never get crazy people anymore.

Ask for what you want from spirit and you will get it!

Large Corporate Psychic Lines

Large corporate psychic lines, like Keen and Liveperson, are operated by companies that conduct nation-wide advertising campaigns and handle a stable of 500 to 1,000 readers or more (not all of them available at the same time, of course). They allow you to set your own per-minute rate, and they generally take 60% or more of the money clients pay to talk to you. In addition, they hold back about 20% of your monthly income for anywhere from four to six months, as a "rolling reserve," to cover potential charge-backs on your calls.

These corporations spend an enormous amount on advertising, and that is how they justify taking such a large cut. The worst of these companies are notorious for hiring anyone who will sign on, regardless of quality, and for not-too-subtly encouraging readers to string out the readings as long as possible. They usually have a huge turnover of readers, so they hire anybody with a pulse. They want the "tell them what they want to hear" type of reader.

The corporate websites usually employ a database-driven algorithm that determines the placement of how readers appear on their website, based on factors such as amount of time logged in per month, how long each reading lasts, how many calls the reader gets per month, and how many clients return for a second or third reading from that reader.

These companies do not allow their readers to contact clients outside of their system, and they do not permit readers to cross-market themselves outside of the corporate website.

Some of these large sites host customer satisfaction rating systems that factor into reader placement, and those rating systems have created havoc when readers have tried to manipulate them to sabotage other reader's listings. As of this writing, that problem has not been solved, so you need to know what you are stepping into if you sign with these companies.

I think it might be great to sign up with one of these services if you need to practice and develop your gifts and skills, but do not consider it a career, or even a livelihood. There are readers who have created careers out of reading this way; they avoid the pitfalls by having an enormous client base they have developed, sometimes over a decade or more. They have such a long track record and such amazing ratings that one or two slams against them just look crazy and have no impact, but this takes an unbelievable amount of diligent time and work!

Also, many readers just can't do work they view as unethical, and find that if they are truthful and efficient with the timing of readings with clients, they are penalized by a system that values "billed minutes" over satisfied clients.

Mid-Size Corporate Psychic Lines

Another type of service is the mid-size psychic line, such as California Psychics or Psychic Source, that lets you set your own per-minute rate and takes a percentage of the fee. The companies that run these mid-size lines may handle 100 to 500 readers. Most of these lines audition their readers to screen for quality, but some don't.

Mid-size lines also use database-driven algorithms for reader placement on their sites, but they are fairer to readers than the big companies and they may also offer their most productive readers a variety of generous benefits and extra promotional opportunities, such as free travel to yearly conferences and access to free professional video and audio services, the results of which are hosted on the readers' pages. Like the big corporate sites, however, they do not allow their readers to contact clients outside of their system, and they do not permit cross-marketing outside of their portal or gateway sites.

Boutique Psychic Lines

Boutique psychic lines, such as Psychic Youniverse, generally handle from 10 to 50 readers. They audition their readers, and they may target specific audiences by offering astrology readings, intuitive life coaching, or some other sub-set within the general psychic field. As with the mid-size lines, the percentage paid to the reader is less than the total paid by the client, and a rolling reserve is held back, but the payout is fair. These lines do not host database-driven ranking systems, and jealousy is at a minimum. Their disadvantages center on low ad budgets and the difficulty of getting a small group of readers to staff the lines 24/7. Unfortunately, some of these sites fake their way around the latter problem by listing "phantom readers" who are never actually online, but make the site look populated.

Readers' Co-op Psychic Lines

The reader's co-op line, such as Hoodoo Psychics, comprises a self-selected group of 10 to 50 readers who pool their resources to create a website and a toll-free phone line, and hire an internet-based call-system to handle their billing for a percentage of the client fees. As with the corporate and boutique lines, a rolling reserve is set aside to cover charge-backs, but the payout to the co-op readers can be as high as 70% of the fees paid by the client, minus phone line charges and incidental expenses, because there is no corporation to take a cut.

The advantages of a co-op line are that all the readers are auditioned and, if the group agrees, the readers can also offer further services to their clients, such as spell-casting, the setting of vigil candles, or sales of spiritual supplies — activities strictly forbidden at other companies. The disadvantages of the co-op system are the difficulty of staffing the line 24/7 and the lack of a large-scale advertising budget. The advertising issue can be addressed without breaking the bank if the members all agree to cross-link ads for the co-op line on their own private websites and social networking pages.

Solo Pre-Scheduled Telephone Reading Services

The internet has levelled the marketing field tremendously, making possible a fourth type of psychic service, the solo-reader's pre-scheduled line. Under this arrangement, the reader does not offer a per-minute billing system, but instead allocates blocks or chunks of time, such as ten-minute, half-hour, and one-hour readings, to clients. The reader verifies the payment before booking the client, so, in effect, this is like booking clients in your office, except that they get their readings over the phone, by Skype, or via email, as you prefer.

Pre-Call Contact for Pre-Scheduled Calls

I like to email the client or have the client email me birth information so I can do a natal chart and I also like to have them email me a list of the questions they will be asking; so that if I have to rephrase the question to assure that the client gets a really useful answer, we are both in agreement about that before the reading. I will email them back a possible rewording of the question. If I'm looking at their natal chart, I can see not only the patterns of recurring problems but I can also see how they hear, how they listen, and I can rephrase what I'm saying so that they get the most value out of the reading.

Ending a Pre-Paid Call

Unlike the per-minute lines, where keeping the client talking makes you money, the pre-paid call system means that if you run overtime, you lose money.

Try to practice a graceful way to end the telephone reading. This is always a tricky point. When I have a client live in front of me I tend to push all my cards together into a stack and ask them "Did you get what you came for? Do you have everything you need from me?" I stand up from the table and that signals that the session is over.

Obviously, on the phone I cannot do this. However, if I have gotten the client's questions via email before the session, I can say, "It looks like we've covered the questions that you specified in your email. We are at the allotted time now. Do you want to go over time? Do you want to ask more questions now, or do you want to wait for another time?"

Or I might say, "Did you get what you came to me for?"

People will keep thinking of questions when you read. More questions always come up for the client, and if you've ever had a reading yourself, you know that feeling. Just as the reader is answering your question, five other questions will pop up in your mind! It doesn't mean the reader didn't answer the question, it just means that one question leads to other questions.

So, as the reader, you are in charge of the show and you have to let people know when the time is up. It is not their responsibility, and you have to find a graceful way to conclude things. How to do that is a very personal choice.

Remember to be there for your clients. That is your purpose. They really need you to be compassionate, kind, and caring, but not to be a doormat. You're like a very kind fairy godmother who manages the time well, is compassionate, does care about clients, and is invested in their growth, not in their dependency. This is true for any kind of reading.

Paypal

Most of the full-time professional readers who do phone work on a solitary or pre-scheduled basis use Paypal to receive payments. All Paypal does is create an easy way to get paid; the marketing of your phone-reading service is still up to you. This will scare off some new readers, especially if they are used to being an employee. Think of it this way: you do have all of the responsibility, but you also have all of the power!

Create a website for yourself and place a Paypal button on it. (I will not tell you how to set this up. Go to Paypal!) Design your web pages with marvellous copy that clearly states what you do and the benefits of having a reading with you. Your web pages will host your Paypal button, making it incredibly easy to book you for a reading. Have your friends visit your site and give you feedback about the ease of navigation and the feel of your site.

Paypal allows clients to ask for a refund and will hold your money until the matter is resolved. I have never had a request for a refund from a client, but in my opinion if somebody requests a refund or says that the reading didn't work for them, or has some other problem, you should refund the money through Paypal at once, and simply not be available to that person in the future. I think this does not happen to me because I do set my intention very powerfully every day before I began my work, and I would recommend that you do the same.

Remember, legally, all callers must be 18 years old to have a phone reading. This will be covered at every group line's website, but if you have a solitary line, you must mention it on your own site. Please be careful about possibly reading for anyone who might be a minor.

Promoting Your Pre-scheduled Phone Service

Google "psychic readings [your city]" and see what comes up. Google "psychic phone readings USA" Notice the directories and maps. Get listed in every directory you can find. Most will be free. Write articles about something related to your phone readings and place them online, with a link leading people to your website. Link a business page about your reading service to your Facebook profile, then add a Twitter feed from the Facebook page.

Join groups and clubs locally and give free talks with funny stories about your work as a reader, and hand out cards with your number and website. You must make yourself high-profile and carve out a niche locally and online so folks will want to call you.

Many local clients will want readings by phone because they are embarrassed to be seen going to a reader, or can't get out of the house easily. They may also have snooping relatives studying Paypal and phone records, so make sure you answer your phone with a business name and have an innocuous-sounding Paypal business name. (You are a consultant!)

As a solitary telephone reader, you will have to do all of your marketing yourself, but it is fun, and there are many terrific books out there on how to do this with a small internet business. It is a process. Do not expect to hang out your shingle and explode with clients.

Schedule Your Available Time

Schedules are important. It might seem like fun to just randomly log on and do phone readings whenever you happen to feel like it, but that is not a productive way to do this kind of work. If you are an employee for a psychic phone line, they will usually demand that you set and keep a specific schedule. The reason they do this is because they have discovered that clients will wait and get a reading from their favourite reader who logs on at a specified time.

If you pay attention to the successful online or telephone readers you will notice that they usually publish a set schedule for the clients to see. This motivates clients to call them for a reading. This also gets back to professionalism, respect, and work ethic. In our business we constantly have to fight the image of the flaky fortune teller, and having a set schedule and the discipline to adhere to it combats the image of a disorganized and unprofessional practitioner.

If you set the intention to work a certain number of hours a day, and if you are actually set up, plugged in, and ready to go during those hours, even if you are not doing readings, the universe will rush to fill those times with the readings and the clients that you intend.

This doesn't happen automatically, but if you are patient and diligent it will. When you first begin and you are sitting waiting for the phone to ring, spend that time usefully, writing articles to publish, working on your website, or working on marketing ideas. If you spend that time reading trashy novels, tempting as that may be, it does not set up the energy for business and will not result in the universe filling your phone line with eager clients.

I initially thought it was a brilliant idea to spend my time as I waited to develop my phone clientele reading all of the classic literature that I had missed out on. I printed out an online list of the top 100 novels of all time, found nearly all of them at my local used bookstore, and piled them all into a basket beside my phone and computer. As soon as I became really engrossed in a story, my phone would ring, and I would be irritable at the interruption. This did not send the correct message to the universe to send me more clients via the phone! When I switched to working on marketing and business plans and projects during the slow times, my phone business exploded.

Advantages and Pitfalls of Reading In Your Pyjamas

Many readers love reading over the phone because they can't be seen and therefore feel a sense of freedom from work-place rules. They can be almost anywhere, as long as the environment is not too noisy, and they can be in any state of dress or undress.

Folks who have spent a good part of their lives dressing up to be at work or having to work in a uniform particularly love the idea of sitting around with a headset strapped on and in their pyjamas lounging about. I personally find that I need to behave as if I am in person seeing the client in order to read for them, just as many folks who become suddenly self-employed and working from home discover that they don't work as well unless they get up and get dressed. The same thing happens when you're a psychic reader. When I'm doing phone readings I am in the same state of dress as if I'm at my office.

If I'm doing phone readings from my home, the home environment I am in has to be tidy, look good and smell good, and be quiet and distraction free, and I have to be completely dressed. Maybe this is just me, but I believe that this has a lot to do with respect for my work, respect for my clients, and respect for myself. The last thing I want to be is the cliché of the grubby, sloppy, pyjama-clad person in a nasty cluttered house giving readings.

An Interview with Gina Thies, A Telephone Reader

Gina Thies is a brilliant tarot reader, teacher, and writer; she composes the "Tarot Tips" newsletter for the New York Tarot School and is a longtime phone reader.

Val: Gina, what made you decide in the first place to do phone readings?

Gina: Well, I started working with the Miss Cleo phone line, and at the time, there really was no other way to do it. That was the technology at the time, you had a dedicated phone line and that was how they connected everybody. I didn't have an office or a place to do readings were I was set up. I was actually thrilled by being able to work in the privacy of my own home where I only had my phone bill and taxes to worry about!

That early phone line was my introduction to reading professionally. I discovered there is a special technique to that type of reading, but because that's how I started, I didn't know any other way to read.

Val: How was it when you first started, in those early days?

Gina: I was really excited that I could actually get paid for this stuff I had studied for so long, and that I wouldn't have to try to drum up business; that someone had already made this into a business. I worked in the corporate world before this, and had a dream about reading professionally. I actually have a degree in fashion illustration!

Reading professionally on the phone was very, very exciting. I was a nervous wreck! I had only read for family and a few friends, so I was nervous about getting it right and very careful about my reputation.

Val: How long did it take you to get over your nerves?

Gina: Well, I have always been a person who has been put out in front of the public, going back to when I was a child in school and in church.

Honestly, the hardest thing was worrying about my reputation and about things like were the clients thinking and saying that I wasn't any good.

The pressure of "I've got to be right" is very difficult. Fortunately, I'm really good under pressure and in crisis. On the phone you have three seconds to tell somebody something where they will go, "Oh!" and stay on the line.

My introduction to reading was from a reader who read like that, so that was the only way that I knew. To jump into the reading and start going right at it like that. But it really is hard to concentrate on the reading while you are worried about if you are good enough and if you are getting the information right. It's not for everyone. But as difficult as it was, I was relatively comfortable from the start because I did feel like I had found my niche. Everything else I had done in my life up until that time had perfectly groomed me for this type of work.

If a person has not dealt with the public much, if they have no experience of being in charge (because that is a big part of managing phone readings!), phone readings will be hard for them. You have to be in charge and work well with the public. I already had that training; I was used to the performance anxiety.

Professional actors will tell you that they will feel nervous before they step out on that stage but it's just something they've got to do. It is instinct and adrenaline. Some people are just not capable of reading in front of a critical audience like that.

Val: So, some people will just not be cut out for phone reading.

Gina: Yes, some people are cut out for this and some are not. And sometimes it's not about fear of being in the public or reading in public; it's about knowing how to communicate and how to handle what's coming back at you and how to manage your ego versus their ego. Some people are excellent with a private client but can't function in this type of arena.

Val: Do you feel that another thing that's very different about phone readings is that there is no visual feedback for the reader?

Gina: Right, the visual cues you get when a person is sitting in front of you are absent.

The thing about it is, to me, and I may be unique in this, but I will go through a process of having them choose a significator. Even if they don't know the suits I will have them pick a playing card.

I have different techniques; sometimes I have them pick a number between 1 and 78, or a number between 1 and 10.

I start reading from that. That tells me right where they are. I never need to see them.

Val: So, are you looking at the numerological significance of the number?

Gina: If I'm doing the 1 through 78, I am starting from the tarot card; obviously you need to know how to count cards well in order to do that quickly!

If I do the 1 through 10, I am using numerology.

Val: Are you doing that to engage the client in the reading, to give them something to do?

Gina: That's part of it, and the energy of the voice is what I'm also picking up. To me energy is energy is energy. We all have certain communication styles. We all have different ways we take in information. For me, reading on the phone is exactly as if the person is right there in front of me. I just read their energy.

Val: From the sound of their voice?

Gina: Yes, just from the sound of their voice.

Val: It is my understanding that a lot of phone readers do that.

Gina: I am very good at just knowing things from hearing the quality of a person's voice. I can tell if there is something they are withholding from me. Perhaps it's because I have had long distance relationships, and frequently been at a distance from my family, so phone was the only contact.

I've traveled a lot and in being at a distance from my children, I can talk to them on the phone and immediately know when something is up! It's just a part of the gift. It is something a reader can pay attention to or not as they choose.

The timing aspect of how long it takes a reader to become comfortable with this sort of work will have much to do with your life experience. Have you dealt much with customer service? Are you good with people? The bottom line, Valentina, is that what you are doing is managing people. I talk about that in the "Tarot Tips" newsletter frequently.

Val: When you started, what were the downsides to working for the psychic lines?

The aspect of only making money when you had the client on the phone. The company actually never said, "Keep the person on the phone as long as possible," however they made it clear that you would get more calls if your timing fell into a certain parameter. So if you could keep your average time up, you simply would get more calls. This was calculated based on how long you kept each individual person on the phone and the percentage of clients who returned to you. I didn't like that. Ethically it bothered me. I wanted to answer the client's questions, but I couldn't fully participate in manipulating the readings to keep people on the phone longer.

Val: Some of these phone services have a chat room and the reader is on video. The guests in the chat room see and interact with the reader, and if they like the reader then sign up for a private session. These services tell the readers to start out at a very low rate per minute, to develop a following, a clientele. What do you think about this?

Gina: That is frustrating to me! I have worked where there is a rate per hour, and then a dollar per email, and then the reader makes half of whatever the reading price is.

I have seen sites where you have to start at this low rate, and it seems to me like it just isn't fair to the reader. I figure I've invested all this time and money and energy in learning my trade, so those very low rates seem a bit insulting. However, it is part of the terrain!

A lot of readers out there are really very good, they have a private practice, they do parties, they have a regular phone clientele. Sometimes they will work on a low-paying phone line just to augment an existing practice, or between scheduled readings. A lot of it is supplemental income. Sometimes the reader has an actual nine to five job.

Val: Oh, I see, I couldn't figure out why anybody would do it! If your private readings are one hundred dollars an hour, why would you work for 99 cents a minute?

Gina: You must decide: Is this a hobby or is this your business? Many hobbyists will be on the cheap phone lines. So you just have to decide what is right personally for you.

Most of the large corporations running the bigger phone lines are only interested in the bottom line, and really don't care about ethics or fairness. It is a business. It is supply and demand, and there are many readers who will read for that cheap rate, especially if it is just a supplemental income for them, so that cheap rate becomes commonplace.

If it doesn't bother you to put a bunch of time in and invest in working your way up to a higher rate and a steady clientele, then do that. It is all about the time.

For me, I never liked the big companies, so I'm not going to be on those lines. I just don't have time. But if you are just starting out and you don't have experience, don't have confidence, and you don't have clientele, corporate phone lines are a great training ground! They are a confidence builder; you get to learn how to deal with the public. That's one reason folks do those kinds of things. But the corporations that own these businesses are just like fast food franchises who hire hourly workers. It's not about spirituality to them, so don't expect them to care about that. Quit expecting these corporations to be different.

There are so many of us out there who want to learn how to successfully work in this business, but are not interested in the non-glamorous aspects. This business is not glamorous! This is a tough business.

A reading is not something that's tangible, and most people are see-it-to-believe-it people. So they will be all, "You have to tell me something that I did when I was in the third grade that I don't even remember," and you have to produce something like that, in order for them to believe you! So, yes, it is a tough business!

If people are spending money, they want to justify to themselves why they are spending that money. For what we do, they need even more justification than usual, because what we do is a non-tangible.

That's why you will constantly get questions like, "Are you good?" "Are you real?" People only want to invest in what they trust in.

Val: What is the most effective style of presentation for reading on the phone?

Gina: As a reader, you walk a really fine line between telling the truth and telling people what they want to hear. You must assess what people are ready to hear and what they are not ready to hear.

A reading at a psychic fair or party is very different from the kind of reading I do in a private phone session. My energy and attitude are the same, but there are certain things I do with a private phone client of mine that I never do in the shorter readings.

I can tend to be really blunt and honest, and sometimes this will discourage people from getting a full session: "Oh no, I don't want to talk to her, she'll tell me the truth!"

I have had clients who would literally sign on to get a reading with me every single day. They would actually wait for me to sign on every single day!

I have had clients who would cycle through a chat room over and over and over again, repeatedly getting tiny short readings from me all day.

What I present to a client depends in part on the regularity of the client and how familiar they are with me.

Val: What do you feel about the guilt some readers express about collecting money for reading, especially when they are advertising a high per-minute rate on the phone?

Gina: If you spend time learning a skill, buying books, going to conferences, why can't you get paid for that? For some reason, many of us do have a hard time with charging fees. We have a hard time with making money. I think you have to look at it like the training a doctor gets, years and years of training. If you invest in yourself, you should get a return on that. Many readers need to look at how they emotionally deal with money.

I still deal with this. When people ask me how much I charge for reading, I will tell them, "Just to go look at my website," rather than directly answering that question. I don't want to deal with it and I don't want to talk about it.

You have to define what financial success is for you. It is very personal.

Interestingly, when you can answer people's questions about your rates with confidence, they seem to be more comfortable with purchasing. If you hesitate, they tend to hesitate. If you just tell them straight out, they tend to say yes.

And the value of a reading can fluctuate in the mind of the client! We hardly ever talk about this. They only see the value when you are right. What if you start being consistently wrong? Where is that going to go? Readers have bad days, like everyone else. I could read for fifty people at a party and be on fire, then that one person sits down and says, "No, no, no" to everything I say.

Val: But, honey, those are the very people who will see you at another party six months down the road and want to Build You A Temple because it all came true!

Gina: I know that, but we are talking about in the moment. Like when they've booked an appointment with you, and to everything you see they say, "No, no, no." And sometimes a reader can be off when they become too close and familiar with the client; they simply know too much about them and are too invested in the outcomes.

Val: That is actually a huge problem! The reader loses perspective and objectivity.

Gina: And if the cards said six months ago that it's a great idea to take that job in Portland, that isn't going to change. The cards reflect every aspect of the human experience, the only variable is what is it and when will it hit your life.

Our life experiences are not that different from the experiences of our ancestors. Your transportation might be a Ferrari instead of a covered wagon, but it is still the experience of transportation. The peripheral things change but human emotions and circumstances do not.

Val: Thank you so much, Gina! I always enjoy talking to you.

A New Convert

David was reading cards at Hotel Zaza, and this lady, who was sort of a Real Texas Gal, about eighty years old and sort of stern, like an ex-schoolteacher, comes up and says, "Let's do this deal!" and sits down at the table. She had what he would call a very staunch personality.

He started reading for her; first doing a layout about the next six months. The reading said something about her moving; the cards clearly said that she would unexpectedly move house in about four months. She would end up landing in a place she would like even better than where she currently lived.

She reached across the table. She grabbed his hand, and she said, "Hon, I'm sure you're really good at what you do, but not one word of that, not one single word of what you just said, applies to me."

We hear this a lot, and I just love these people!

David replied to what she said, by saying, "Ma'am, not to be disagreeable, but it's the future. Come back in six months and tell me how wrong I am."

So, fast-forward six months later.

David was reading at the hotel one night. And she comes busting down the hallway. He sort of recognized her, but he reads for so many people that he frequently doesn't remember them.

He was in the middle of reading for a couple and she actually interrupted the reading.

He thought, "Oh, God. Here we go. She's gonna tell these people I'm awful, just full of crap." That has never happened, but it seems we always question ourselves so much that we're always expecting it! (I think you're probably not a very good reader if you aren't constantly questioning the authenticity of what you do.) We are always astonished at how accurate reading is; we never expect it to be as powerful and as right-on as it is.

She interrupts and says, "I'm sorry; I know you're busy working. I have to tell you: everything you said to me, and I don't know how, because there's no way you could've known, came true! I moved exactly when you said I would move, and I love the house I am in. There's no way you could've known that, because I didn't know it. I just want you to know that I'm apologizing right now."

She threw a twenty-dollar bill down on the table and shook the hand of the person sitting in one of the seats: "You take notes and you listen to every word he says! He knows what he's talking about!"

Marketing Yourself

Marketing changed my life.

I believe it is possibly the most important piece of the puzzle when it comes to creating your business.

It's not difficult to create a busy practice as a reader, but it is extremely easy to fall into the trap of creating a busy practice that feels like a real job, a job you do not like!

As readers, we see via the stories of our clients how easy it is to unconsciously fall into a pattern, especially a negative one.

It must be basic human nature.

A new reader will hang up a shingle, figure out the easiest and most inexpensive physical space to do readings, and throw open the doors to all comers. If this freshly minted reader has had a "real job" prior to this, there will be the intoxicating expectation of the imagined freedoms and pleasures of sole proprietorship.

If you check back with that new reader 24 months later, you will probably see someone in the first stages of burn-out. The reader will procrastinate about returning phone calls and emails, get a heavy feeling before sessions with clients, will joke in a bitter and cynical way about clients, and will have begun to hate the work that was so promising and beloved such a short time before.

That new reader had the opportunity and power to create work that occurred any way they could have imagined, yet fell into the trap of designing it to feel exactly like a real job.

A truly oppressive real job!

What happened here?

What happened was the new reader started business without a clear marketing plan.

Most folks think a marketing plan is only for a big company. Why would a small sole practitioner in a service business need such a thing? Can't you just start working?

If you begin without a marketing plan, it is like stepping into a marriage without having those all-important conversations about the big issues. A marketing plan acts like a fantastic relationship counsellor, facilitating conversations and agreements about boundaries, expectations, roles, and communication.

I know it sounds odd to think of your new business as a person you would have a relationship with, but that really is how it is!

Your Ideal Day

Begin imagining your ideal day as a reader. When do you start? How do you prepare for your client? Where do you hold your readings? When do you take breaks? When do you do phone call and email time? How many clients do you want to see in a day?

As you imagine this, really pay attention to the feelings you experience as you go through this imaginary day. Pay attention and notice any times in your imaginary day where you make assumptions about how it has to be, or where you quickly gloss over what is happening. Once you imagine all the pieces of your ideal day, deconstruct it.

Write out each activity on a separate index card. Now, move them around.

Play with your idea of what has to happen and when it has to happen. Remove any of the cards that give you an unhappy feeling. Pay attention to them. Ask yourself important questions such as, "Why does this make me uncomfortable?" and "What am I avoiding?"

Playing around with these pieces of your day at this point will save you a lot of grief later on. You may discover that your ideal day includes a long, relaxed, luxurious lunch followed by a brief nap. Instead of deciding that this is inappropriate and self-indulgent, see if perhaps allowing yourself the luxury of this type of schedule will put you in such a fantastic and receptive mood that you can better serve your clients when they show up for afternoon and evening sessions with you. (Please note that this is simply an example, I am not suggesting that every reader requires a siesta to be effective. These are meant to be very personal choices.)

Many new readers just throw open the doors and are so happy to have a client at all that they schedule appointments whenever the client wishes, and fill up their schedule as much as possible. New readers may forget how important it is to take care of and respect themselves.

If you nourish yourself by setting powerful boundaries around sleep, food, family, and recreation, you will show up as powerfully present in your sessions with clients. A part of your spirit will not be feeling resentful and neglected because you are hungry, need to pee, and didn't get enough sleep. These things matter, and they affect the quality of your work!

Pick Your Clients

Describe your favourite client right now, and that is probably your niche client or your ideal client, and the subjects you primarily work on with them are probably the niche you should fill, the specialty you should address as a reader.

Where are other people like this person?

Once you know the kind of clients that you like, the ones you prefer, the next action is to figure out what they really want, what they want more than anything, what most of them are coming to you for. Then consider what you like to do the most, what you find to be the most interesting kind of work in this field.

When you realize that you are really in charge of how you spend your days and who you spend them with, life becomes much more interesting. The kind of work we do is fun and interesting and amazing, but it can really get to be a drag if you are not enjoying the clients and their stories, and enjoying helping them get to where they want to go.

Maybe your most exciting client is the mid-life entrepreneur just beginning to launch a business. If you let your office and your days be filled with whiny young gals endlessly complaining about their love lives, you will not be having fun; in fact you will be miserable. You probably will not have as many clients as you want either, because clients can sense your joy and passion, or lack of it.

If you choose the entrepreneurs as your niche clientele, decide what it is you do for them and how to explain it in a very concise way; figure out where they congregate, what they read, what associations they belong to, and show up in those areas (physically or with advertising) telling them what you can do for them, and you will be a success.

Or perhaps you like reading for young college women — intelligent, hopeful, ready to meet life and all it offers. If you waste your time reading for broken down alcoholics, you won't have time to read for those college girls and make a wonderful difference in their lives.

If you choose the college girls, use wording at your website that mentions both career and love, and present yourself as a friendly and insightful mentor. They will seek you out.

Get rid of the crappy people, the clients that you don't like, anybody that makes you feel uncomfortable or seems faintly disrespectful of you, all of the tire kickers and the guess-my-weight jerks. You do not need them. You'll actually have a larger and better-paying clientele when you stop letting these people suck up your time and energy.

Branding!

My personal favourite topic in marketing!

Branding is fun, because branding is all about deciding who you are and then clearly communicating that to your audience. Working on your branding is one of the most creative projects you will ever attempt. Branding is creatively figuring out who you are in the arena of your business, and involves asking these important questions:

- What do you stand for?
- What is so special about you?
- What makes you different from every other practitioner?
- Why should a client choose you rather than your competition? (Note: Never make this choice about price. If you compete based on price, being cheaper than your competition, you will be very disappointed to discover that clients do not seek out readings or other types of spiritual service based on price.)
- What is exciting about you and your services?
- What are your specialities in terms of divination tools?
- How would you describe your style of reading? (Experiment with terms like "insightful," "direct and honest," "compassionate," "fun," "hard-hitting," "uplifting," and "gifted;" choose as many as you feel comfortable with and discard the rest.)
- Who do you want to help?
- What are you going to help them do?
- How are you going to accomplish this?
- Why is this work important to you?

Answering these questions will take a little work.

You will have to set aside some time so that you can think through this. It is not something you can figure out in an afternoon. Don't procrastinate!

Branding yourself is quite possibly the most important part of your entire business, and the future success of your whole career in this business rests upon clear and authentic choices based upon the answers to these questions. If you have to take some time away from home and family and social obligations in order to concentrate clearly upon answering these questions, do that!

Remember also that branding yourself may extend to encompass such seemingly peripheral æsthetic choices as the predominant colours at your website, the way you decorate your office, and even the type fonts on your business cards and brochures.

Marketing Basics

Here are the bare basics you'll need for any kind of marketing:
- A website
- A phone
- A professional email address
- Professional photos
- Quality business cards
- Testimonials from clients

Your Web Site

If you do not have a website, you do not exist professionally.

Having a website is more important than having business cards.

The internet is how everybody finds everything these days, and you cannot afford to not be searchable. No matter how you decide to approach your career as a reader, whether you are more interested in the counseling and wellness approach or consider yourself a public entertainer, this is a basic necessity.

Inexpensive website hosting packages can be had for just a few dollars a year, complete with professional email addresses, and built-in site design templates.

Make the landing page (the first page someone hits when they come to your website) very clear, understandable, and easy to navigate. It's especially important that there be an obvious and simple way to contact you for a reading. All of the descriptive writing on your landing page needs to be about what the potential client gets when they get a reading from you, instead of a bunch of metaphysical jargon and an explanation of how awesome you are. I am sure you are awesome, but a potential client landing on your website just really wants to know which of their problems you can solve, how you can do that, and how much it will cost.

Your Phone

Get a good phone, and answer it when it rings.

When clients call you, they are in the mood to purchase your services. If you make them wait and call them back later, they may have moved on to another reader or they may have had a change of heart about having a reading at all. Most clients will call a reader when they are at a critical juncture and want relief and answers immediately. Even if you consider yourself primarily a party and event reader, the host or event planner who is calling you wants to get the entertainment nailed down for the party so they can move on to other things.

I have had all sorts of issues with staying on top of my phone calls, for as long as I can remember. I have always been juggling several projects at once, and the phone always seemed like a rude interruption of those projects. I decided to change my mind and attitude about this, and when I did that, the success of my business changed.

Now, I schedule an hour to an hour and a half between client sessions, just so I can return phone calls and emails. That means I usually return phone calls within the hour, at the latest. This has improved my business more than anything else I have ever done!

Also, do not have a long, junky, and annoying voice-mail message. Nobody wants to hear your musical choices or your child's squeaky voice when they call.

A Professional Email Address

A professional looking email address that is simple and easy to remember is a necessity.

Your email address should be located at the same domain-name as your website. (Mine is admin@valentinaburton.com.) As stated earlier, many website packages come with several free email addresses included, and they usually end in ".com," which is what you want. Avoid silly, goofy, sexy, or indecipherable email addresses. You may be in an unusual business, but you need to look like a serious and trustworthy business person.

Professional Photos

One of the first things you need to do when setting up your business is to contact a photographer and have some professional headshots done. You will use these photos on your website and on your business cards and brochures.

Potential clients want to see you. They do not want to see a drawing of a gypsy fortune teller or an artsy photo of hands with tarot cards, a crystal ball, white doves, etc.

People want to know who they are doing business with, and our business is one where we really need to engender trust in our potential clients.

If you pay attention, you'll notice that storefront "neon-readers" and their internet counterparts almost never use photos of themselves, because, in fact, there usually is more than one person portraying "Sister Anna" or "Psychic Mrs. Smith" in their businesses. Such readers prefer to employ generic photo-service images like the hands on the crystal ball.

I think it's very important to distance yourself from those kinds of readers, to make it clear that the service you offer is of a much higher quality. One way to make that higher level of quality very clear is to have excellent photos of yourself all over your marketing materials, so you are communicating that you, a real person, stand behind your business.

Quality Business Cards

Business cards are not the most important part of your marketing arsenal, but they are very useful. If you sell products with your service, tuck a business card into every outgoing package. You may also place cards at cafes and metaphysical shops, with permission.

Have a professional photo taken to go on your card, and write out copy for your card that is simple, elegant, and to the point. Please do not use clip art. Your photo, professional name, phone number, website URL, email address, and a couple of lines about what you do should all be on your card. Never put your home address on your business card.

Thin and cheaply printed cards, free cards from a printing service that include the printing service's name on the back, or worse, cards that you print up yourself with your computer, will do nothing to bring you clients. It is better to have no cards than to have cards that look cheesy. Order the finest and heaviest card stock you can get. I promise you, those flimsy business cards just get tossed in the trash, but people will hang on to an attractive, substantial, and interesting card.

For a couple of years I made up some really special business cards that were heavy and shiny, and had a lucky charm coin (which I had minted up by a token company) glued on the front. That was over five years ago, and I still run into people who will open their purse or wallet and pull out one of those cards with the lucky coin attached!

Testimonials From Clients

The final things you absolutely must have are glowing testimonials from happy and satisfied clients! They are solid gold. This is another thing that the "neon" readers cannot hope to compete with, as they will frequently either leave clients feeling frightened, uneasy, and faintly ripped off, or they have actually ripped off a client by running a scam and have skipped town. (So they are never around long enough to collect any testimonials.)

If you are just beginning and you really don't have any clients yet to give you glowing testimonials, do a charity event in exchange for a lovely testimonial from the organizer.

Do some readings at a party. There are always a couple of guests who are just astounded at how "right on" and how much fun getting a reading is, and usually those folks want to hand you a tip. When they offer the tip to you, have a little notebook handy where they can scribble down a testimonial for you instead. Don't ask people for their full actual names, some people are sensitive about this, just ask for their initials to accompany the testimonial.

Once you have decided on your niche and your purpose, you will want to cultivate testimonials that speak about how you solved the exact problem the client needed. For example, if you want to specialize in love readings you will want primarily testimonials that say something about how much fun it was to see you, how you put her mind at ease about her relationship, and now she is getting married to him next month!

Have testimonials right on your landing page, do not hide them away on a separate page. You want clients to see them immediately and not have to click again to see those awesome words from your happy and satisfied clients.

Do not, under any circumstances, make up fake testimonials. Fake testimonials always look fake. They are obvious. Just don't go there!

An Interview with Mistria Langlois, A Successful Self-Marketer

Mistria Langlois was an acquaintance of several years who was at an interesting turning point in her life when she sat down with me in my office on a sweltering Texas summer day a few years back. She had worked primarily in the music industry and the corporate world, and really didn't feel like she belonged there anymore, but wasn't sure what to do next. In two hours on that day, I sketched out a business and marketing plan for her new business as a card reader, then we went and had a lovely Italian lunch.

My experience has been that frequently you can hand somebody a roadmap to success, but their own inertia will stop them from pursuing it.

Not Mistria! She took everything I gave her that day and ran with it.

I could not be more proud of the success she has achieved if I had done it myself!

This is an interview I did with her at the Dallas Psychic Fair in April of 2011:

Val: Mistria, when we had our little pow-wow, we sat down and took a couple of hours that afternoon, and I said here is how you put together a practice as a psychic, and what was marvellous was you actually went and did it!

Mistria: This is true!

Val: Most people would not. So, the main question I had was what was the most useful thing or things from that little afternoon pow-wow?

Mistria: Ah, so many things! One of the biggest things, which was so funny because you wouldn't think it would be so big: I had told you everything in my life was a nine, in numerology. I had no attachments, had a hard time hanging on to money, etc., and you told me, "You know what? Just change everything to an eight."

And you can't believe what a huge difference that made! I created the professional name with an eight, the website with an eight; and within a week I had income coming in!

So, then I found it really funny because a week after that I went to a seminar, and they had a raffle. I entered and instead of my real name put Mistria, my new professional name, on the raffle ticket. I never win anything in raffles, but I won a book and all sorts of things!

Every time I put "Mistria" on something I win. That has never happened to me before!

It changed my focus, it seemed to change everything. Everything I do with the name Mistria seems to have the Midas touch. I just can't lose!

And it was just being able to make that shift and realize that I didn't have to live with what I was born with that I could change it. For me, knowing that fact was huge!

Val: So you used numerology to select a professional name, and made it an eight because the number eight is about prosperity and abundance and good business.

I do recommend this, even though it can be sort of hard to work out. My first name adds up to an eight, and my first and last names together also add up to an eight.

Mistria: Yes, even with Chinese numerology it is the same for eight, all about prosperity.

Val: That is really funny! And marvellous!

Mistria: And with the business plan, knowing what to look for and also to know that if I did come across a problem I could call you and ask you, "What do I do?"

Val: That is huge, and I do that with my teachers and mentors. I called one yesterday, because I had a very strange situation, so I called her for advice. It's fantastic to have that.

I think having a coach or mentor in any business is a necessity. I think it's important to be fearless about asking someone to be a coach or mentor. The worst thing they can do is say no, and they will probably only say no because of time constraints.

Most people love coaching and mentoring. It's very fun and stimulating for the coach! When you do something for a long time, you don't even know anymore everything that you know; mentoring someone reminds you of all those things. It's really fantastic to be mentored and coached, too.

Mistria: It allows you the confidence to move forward and not hold yourself back. You know that if you hit a wall you have someone there to help you.

Val: I think a big problem for a lot of readers initially is fear. But you are more likely to step into what's new and be more fearless about it because you don't feel like you are doing it all alone!

So, the thing I notice about you, and the reason I think you actually did what I sat down and told you to do, is you have a fearless and energetic approach (and that is putting it mildly!) to cold calling potential clients and potential venues.

Mistria: Many of the things I've experienced in my life previously have helped me be able to do this. I worked Renaissance Fairs; I've been in the music business, things like that. I learned a lot about entertainment and event production from the Renaissance Fairs.

But what is interesting is I was never a performer! I was always booking other acts or putting other acts on the stage. I really never cared about the performing part, I much preferred being behind the scenes. So I can easily talk to club owners, it's old hat for me. I can talk to people who are famous, I'm never star struck. So, if I know what I'm talking about I have no problem, but I can't sell something I don't like or sell something from a sales script. It's interesting because it's absolutely harder to sell yourself, but I have no trouble doing this!

There a lot of readers that are better readers than me or have been doing it longer, but I have more of the entertainment aspect going for me and experience in the entertainment industry, so I don't have those fears about just calling someone and presenting an idea and asking for what I want.

Val: That is wonderful, so creative! You took something that actually was a problem, a limitation, and used it to find a solution that made something which was much more fun.

Mistria: Yes!

Val: What advice would you give someone who is just beginning, particularly in the area of marketing, in this type of business?

Mistria: Well, that depends! There are two basic directions to go in this business, the counseling and wellness approach, or presenting readings as entertainment.

I think readers need to get very clear about how they see themselves and what they want to do. It's all about desire. They could start by thinking about how they see themselves working in a year or two. Do they want to do private and phone readings, or are they primarily interested in the public and entertainment aspect of readings?

I would have to say that deciding on this is the most important thing — deciding if they want to be a public or a private reader.

Do you want a steady gig? What kind of area do you want to read in? Do you want to do parties and events? Would you prefer reading privately or over the phone?

You might have to actually try all of those things and see how they feel to you. You have to be okay with the idea of trial and error. Everything will not work, and that is okay!

Once you decide what you want, then just go out and do it.

Val: I agree. That is the place to start from! In fact, you can't really develop any kind of marketing plan until you have a clear idea of whom and what you want to be.

You have made such a great success in such a short time, and you do everything with such energy and such a great attitude!

Thank you for taking the time with me today!

Guess My Weight

A group of couples stroll down the hall at the hotel and seem very curious about us. As they go by, an older woman in the group points at me and asks David, "Is she Gypsy?"

David, not wanting to be indelicate, replies, "She's American, she's mixed."

Much later, a woman from the group returns to my table and signs up for a reading.

She sits down, and folds her arms across her chest. "My mother does this, and I'm psychic too. We're Gypsy, the real thing. Do you remove curses and bring back lost loves? How about giving me a professional discount on this reading?"

"This is the discounted price," I reply.

"Okay, okay."

"What would you like to ask the cards?"

"All right, how many children do I have?"

I can't help it. I say, "don't you know?"

"I'm just testing you, to see if you're any good."

In this uncomfortable moment, a sudden calm comes over me, and it seems as if my cards are saying, "Trust us, we won't let you down. Let us deal with this woman. Just Trust."

I hope I'm not losing my mind, but decide to let go of worrying about being right.

I begin to read.

"Your eldest is a boy, upper-elementary-school age, who thinks he is smarter than you and is getting away with some sneaky stuff, so you better watch him. Next, you have twin girls, early-elementary-age. One of them is very Disney Princess, the other is athletic, smart, a real leader. You will be most proud of her. To answer your question, you have three children."

Only then do I look up at the woman's face. She is pale. Leaning forward, she whispers, "See that man over there? He's my husband. Please will you answer one more question for me, a real question this time? Is he cheating on me?"

I let out my chatty little cards once more.

The cards said that he was thinking about cheating, yet hadn't actually acted upon it.

She quietly left, and we have never seen any of them again.

I know it's a terrible tarot cliché, but just trust your cards! If someone is confrontational and you have to read for them, just say what you see.

You will be even more amazed than your client!

SOUVENIR DE LA
" Reine des Voyantes "

Marketing Your Career

If you want to quickly create a vibrant and fun business for yourself, you will have to go beyond the basics of simply marketing your readings and market your entire career. Career marketing can be done by creating a devoted fan following, by advertising, or by a combination of both. Here are some career marketing strategies to consider:

- Teach classes at a local metaphysical or occult shop
- Practice regular social networking via Facebook, internet forums, and Twitter
- Develop a monthly newsletter via email or print
- Create a blog, and blog frequently
- Start a Youtube channel or a Blog Talk Radio show
- Issue press releases
- Send out direct mail pieces
- Cultivate speaking engagements
- Write an article, a regular column, or a book
- Get listed in both free and paid directories
- Establish cross-promotions with a complementary business
- Use pay-per-click advertising

Social Networking

Make a Facebook profile and from it create a page for your reading business. Acquire 25 "likes" on the business page and you can then claim your business name at Facebook.

Create a Twitter account, then link your Twitter feed from your Facebook page. Post at least three times a week, and if you read for a co-op phone line, post a message every time you go online! Upload new pictures in groups of no more than three at a time.

Join forums for the discussion of tarot, palmistry, or astrology. These are great places to showcase your knowledge and your personality and tell folks how to find you— but be aware that forum discussions can get heated, and a moment of fury can undo years of reputation-building, so only enter the forums if you can stay cool, calm, and collected.

A Monthly Newsletter or Blog

Use the email lists you develop though social networking to send out a monthly email newsletter. Constant Contact is currently the best service for this type of marketing.

Start a text blog, but also consider video-blogging some sample readings to Youtube, or audio-blogging readings at Blog Talk Radio. Publicize your blog entries via Facebook.

Teaching and Lecturing

Perhaps the easiest and most traditional of the career-enhancing strategies listed above is to teach classes in tarot. Many metaphysical and occult shops encourage after-hours teaching sessions at their premises to draw customers, and if you actively help them sell their tarot decks, they will welcome your classes. Clients like to feel proud of their readers, and knowing that "my reader is a teacher" increases your prestige in their eyes.

An Interview with Major Tom Schick,
A Tarot Teacher and Lecturer

Major Tom Schick is an example of a reader who has become a well-known tarot teacher, lecturer, and publisher (his annual "Tarot Lover's Calendar" has been an ongoing success since 2002). I interviewed him in March, 2012.

Val: Tom, how have teaching tarot, participating in online forums, and publishing enhanced your success?

Tom: Teaching and lecturing have actually become some of my favourite activities! I particularly enjoy teaching beginners tarot because it's just so much fun! I get to watch the light come on, and there's hardly anything more fun than that. As far as enhancing the career, it's certainly helped me professionally. People know me because I've been to conferences and given talks or lectures. It's a chance to contact a wider audience.

Val: Do you think teaching and lecturing places you in another category, makes you seem different from someone who has simply hung out their shingle as a reader?

Tom: Absolutely! And another thing teaching has certainly done for me is teach me new things. I learn something new every time I teach a class. I deepen my own understanding. So, it is a learning process for me as well. Does that make me a better reader? Of course it does. Also, students who have taken my course will then go out and talk about it; it has a sort of snowball effect.

Val: What's your idea of the perfect class size?

Tom: Small enough for individualized attention, but big enough for some fun dynamics between the students. I like to balance somewhere in between six and ten. To me, that creates the ideal class size.

Val: Do you have any tips on what to teach, and how much to teach in a single class session? What is enough to feel juicy, and what is just too much? I have a real problem with that, I always just cram too much in.

Tom: There are some people who offer two-hour sessions over a course of several weeks, and there are others who will cover the same total material over one weekend. My course is twenty hours over a series of weeks. I prefer shorter time blocks because it takes time to integrate the knowledge. Tarot is such a large and broad topic that it is easy to cogitate all over your students and baffle them. You can give them too much in one go.

Val: Yes, I've done that!

Tom: Some people do learn well that way; they like to take in lots of material all at once. However I think most people need a little more time.

Val: It seems like it doesn't stick as well, as if there is a natural limit to what someone can absorb all at once. More than that seems to sort of just bounce off.

Tom: Exactly.

Val: How do you advertise, how do you let people know about your classes?

Tom: I've tried newspaper and magazine adverts, I've tried online advertising, I've tried newsletters, I've tried all sorts of things!
The most effective advertising for my classes has been putting up posters at the local supermarket and at the library, dropping off postcards at the local metaphysical shop, and putting up notices everywhere there is a community notice board. That has been the most effective for me.

Val: Do you give out handouts with your classes? Printed materials?

Tom: I keep my handouts to a minimum.
I distribute a handout to begin with that has the class schedule on it, so students know the details of class times, and so forth. I then give them handouts with very brief descriptions of the trumps, as well as worksheets on the pips and the court cards.
There isn't a bunch of information on the handouts, but we use the handouts during the course for the students to take their own notes.

Val: Do the students retain the information better if they write it out on the handouts?

Tom: Well, the way I teach tarot to my students involves them finding their own meanings for the cards, so I make them write those things down.

Val: What is typical to charge for tarot classes? I'm pretty sure that varies wildly.

Tom: There are places to learn for free, there are places where you can spend hundreds of dollars. What you charge in part depends on what you feel comfortable with.
When I first offered my class, it was 50 pounds ($80.00) for twenty hours. I practically gave it away! Now I m up to 120 pounds ($190.00), which is still fairly cheap.
I think a class is worth more to people if they have to pay a bit.

Val: They might actually show up and pay attention, they will feel it has more value. Do the students pay at each class? Do they pay half to begin? How do you structure that?

Tom: I have always offered a choice. They can pay so much up-front or by the first lesson, or if they want to spread the cost, it is a little more expensive, but they can pay me weekly. So, it is their choice is to pay the total up-front or weekly.

Val: How is lecturing different from teaching?

Tom: The only real difference is the sophistication of the audience about the subject.

When you are lecturing, you are talking to people who are already in the business in some way or another. Even if they are relatively new, if they are at a conference, they already know how to read the cards. You are offering something more than the basic knowledge.

Val: How does someone get to lecture at a conference? How does that work?

Tom: You can put yourself forward to conference organizers, let them know what you would like to present. Or, they can approach you. When I went to Melbourne, I put myself forward for that. I came up with a topic for a three-day workshop, six hours, on creating your own tarot deck, which was good fun!

Val: In addition to using teaching and lecturing as marketing tools, you also participate in online forums. How can forums positively affect a reader in a marketing context?

Tom: By participating in forums, you are effectively creating a persona. This is how other people come to know you and what you stand for. The nature of online forums includes debates and conflicts, so how you conduct yourself during those debates and conflicts defines you for other members of the forum. Forums can be difficult if you are a prickly person.

Recently, many of the older tarot forums have lost members to tarot groups on Facebook. The Facebook groups seem to have less of an agenda and are more wide-open. There is less editing of ideas in the Facebook tarot groups.

Val: Are forums something to participate in more with an objective of eventually lecturing rather than teaching?

Tom: The participants in a forum are going to be from every end of the spectrum. Even folks who might be mildly curious about the topic are going to find the forum. It's a kind of socializing space where they are going to want to be able to share their knowledge as well.

Val: It seems the value of doing these things is the stamp of prestige it gives you, the ability to communicate who you are and what you stand for. The forums and groups are about making yourself available so people can get to know you, that is their marketing value.

Tom: Yes, to know you, to know what you know, to share your unique take on the subject. People are more likely to listen to what you have to say if you have done these things.

Val: Is there anything else you would be willing to share about these topics?

Tom: Yes, teaching isn't for everybody! Either you can communicate ideas well to others in a way that they can absorb and use, or you can't. Some people just can't do it. So, it's not a route for everyone.

If you are a person who has trouble standing up in front of a group and speaking, then you are going to struggle trying to teach a tarot course because that's what you have to do! It's very much a try-it-and-see-if-it-works sort of thing. Not everyone is cut out for teaching.

Val: This is great! Thank you for this interview!

Off the Top of My Head

I have always been a fan of anything theatrical. David and I religiously abide by the Bob Mackie Rule "why use two when you can use twenty." We are native Texans who really believe in the Texas idea of Go Big Or Go Home. So, we never do simple costumes. We are always looking for ways to be more fabulous. I'm pretty sure I spent a former life as a drag queen. I am very short, and since I am a card reader, I am usually seen from the tabletop-up, so I tend to prefer fancy turbans with plenty of height when I dress for events.

A few years ago, I was booked to do a Bat Mitzvah that had a glitzy theme. I knew the family of the lovely young girl the party was celebrating, and I wanted my part of her celebration to be as nice as possible. I decided to create a marvellous feathered headdress in the colours of her party, something so spectacular that it would be unforgettable.

The Bat Mitzvah was perfect. Everything from the caterer, to the deejay, to the décor was exactly as planned. I read the cards for everyone there, young and old, and I had as much fun as the guests.

The family wanted me to stick around after the party ended, to do a special reading just for the honouree, and of course I was happy to oblige. She sat across from me, glowing like a very young Liv Tyler. The deejay and caterers were loading out, the lights were up, and the event space had that sad, romantic feel that a theater has after a show has finished. The family sat clustered behind her in quiet anticipation as I began to read her cards.

I jumped into the reading enthusiastically. I noticed her face registering surprise, and (I thought) delight. The family behind also looked a bit stunned and surprised, I thought they must be fascinated with my accuracy! I continued babbling away, and they kept glancing at each other, beginning to look uncomfortable. A small voice piped up from the back "Your HAT!" I wasn't sure what that meant, so I paused to take a breath. "FIRE!" I was still confused, so I laughed.

"NO, REALLY…YOUR HAT IS ON FIRE!"

In a flash, I finally registered what had happened and yanked the turban off of my head and tossed it onto the cement floor, then doused the flaming feathers with the contents of my water glass. In my excitement I had bobbed my head too close to my tall candlesticks and ignited my spectacular feathers. It wasn't exactly the sort of drama I had intended to create, but it certainly made the party memorable!

"ZADA"
SUPER SECOND - SIGHT STAR.

Legal

Starting a business as a psychic, tarot reader, palmist, or any other type of divination professional really isn't complicated or difficult. The hardest part usually is recognizing the gifts, learning the skills, and polishing the talents enough so that you are sure you are offering a really great product. There's not much wiggle-room for mediocrity in our business (contrary to popular public opinion!), meaning that even a slightly sloppy or inept professional in another field can usually earn a living, and that is not so with us.

Even if you are eager to hang out your shingle, take a little time to consider how you wish to structure yourself legally, as a business.

This requires (of course) having the sorts of conversations with yourself that I suggested in the chapter on marketing: Who do you want to be? What do you want to do?

Taxes

Most professional readers begin their business careers as a "sole proprietor," which means the reader is the sole business owner, and is completely responsible for everything the business does. In the United States, if you do not legally file to change your business to something else, this is the default setting.

As a sole proprietor, your business does not have a separate tax return from you. Your Social Security number is the tax number for the business. On your tax return, you simply figure the profit or loss, take your deductions, and pay the IRS your self-employment tax.

If you are self-employed in the United States, you have to estimate the amount of tax you will have to pay every year, divide that into four payments, and pay this amount to the IRS every quarter. If you dump every penny you make into your business checking account, it is much easier and much more organized. Once you begin to show a profit, you can pay yourself.

See to it that you always leave twenty percent of your income in your business checking account, so you always have an amount in there to pay your IRS quarterlies; or you can set up a separate savings account and place money in there regularly to cover those quarterly payments. It's a pain in the neck, but it's still much better than being someone's employee!

You only need to get a separate tax ID number (an Employer Identification Number or EIN) for your business if you choose to have employees. Having employees gets complicated, due to the need for withholding taxes. It's much easier to set your business up so everybody whom you hire to help you is legally defined as an independent contractor.

If this seems too complicated, hire a CPA and delegate all of this mess to the professional! You do have better things to do; a good CPA can transform your life.

Incorporation

As your business grows, it's probably going to be a fantastic idea to incorporate.

Legal incorporation means that you are setting up your business as a separate entity from yourself. If someone sues you, or there is some other difficulty with the business, your private assets are protected.

Every state has different peculiarities in their laws about incorporating. You can hire an attorney to help you incorporate, or find kits and computer programs to do this yourself.

Local Licensing Laws

Before you begin your business, go online to your city or county's website. There usually will be some sort of a search box. Search under terms like "special permits psychic," "zoning psychic," "special permit astrology," etc. You are checking to see what the local laws are and if you will have to get a special permit or a business license in order to practice.

I have my office in the large metropolitan city of Dallas, and my home is less than a mile away, in a northern suburb. The city that I live in requires a special permit to do anything like a psychic business, and it is nearly impossible to get one of those special permits. Dallas doesn't care and requires nothing special, which is why I office there.

If you have physical products to sell, you may need to register for a vendor's license or a resale license. In my state these are issued by the state government, not by the county or the city. Check your area and see what is necessary for you.

Always put "For Entertainment Purposes Only" on your website and advertising. Clients know that this is not true, so it doesn't run off any potential business for you, but it is supposed to add a layer of legal protection, and in some areas of the country it is required by law, so, since websites are seen nationwide, it is a good idea to use this disclaimer.

An important tool to use to protect yourself legally is to get an ordination or a minister's license. It's very easy to get ordained on the internet; some sites only ask that you send in a little money, and you are good to go. Other sites offer a course of study whereby you earn your ordination. This is not necessary, although it can be interesting, and if you learn some effective counseling techniques, an ordination course will help you to be a better reader.

Ordination is a little like auto insurance. The basic idea is this: if you have an ordination, you can be doing our kind of work and you are completely protected under the Constitution. Nobody can challenge you and cause you trouble by saying that you are "counseling without a license" or some other nonsense. You are an Ordained Minister doing spiritual counseling. The peace of mind of having this is worth every single penny!

Your DBA

Once you decide on a business name, you will need to register it. This is called getting a DBA, which means "Doing Business As." You must have a DBA to set up a checking account in your business name, if your business name is different from your own legal name. Call your county administration offices to determine where to go to register the DBA.

I have always considered the date that I register the DBA to be the astrological birth date of my business, so I have always chosen those dates very carefully. Every business, and every person, has ups and downs; but I also believe choosing a name that carries great numerology for success is a good practice! Make sure to cross-check the astrological and numerological compatibility between you, the business birth date, and the business name. It's possible to select the numerology and astrology to create a strong, vibrant, and profitable business, but have it become a business that you dislike.

Once you have your DBA, then you can go and set up a checking account in your business name. It may seem to be too much complication if you are simply planning to be a sole proprietor, but it really helps you to keep things organized.

Another Night of Glamour at Hotel Zaza

My assistant David and I lay out our reading table on a sultry Texas evening.

Before we can get all of the table fabrics arranged and candles lit, an intoxicated, big haired, abundantly siliconed young woman lands in the client's chair.

"What is this?"

"I'm the House Fortune Teller; I read tarot cards."

"Really? My pastor says that's wrong! How can you do something that's evil like that? That's just wrong! You're serving Satan!" (hiccup)

"I certainly respect your opinion, and your pastor's opinion. I think he's right, this probably isn't for you."

David, to force her hand and get her out of the chair asks, "Would you like a reading?"

She is horrified. "I could never do that! Jesus hates fortune tellers!"

She points at David and says, "Who's he, your pimp?"

I say, "David works with me. He keeps track of who's next and takes care of the guests."

Then she says, "I want a reading! Sign me up, Mr. Pimp, but you have to go away, because you scare me."

David actually looks like he might agree to those terms, as long as she pays up front. He's a very practical Taurus.

I respond with, "I'm so sorry, I just can't in good conscience read for you. I won't be a party to you compromising your high moral and spiritual principles."

She's shocked. "But you have to! You have to because I want it!"

Remember, you are a free agent and you always have the right to politely refuse service as you choose. If you plan on reading in a business or public place, you are unlikely to be an actual employee. However, your interaction with everyone must be above reproach, and your standards of behaviour are higher than expected of the employees. People will try to bait you and get you to argue. You do not have to participate. Don't engage and don't be defensive.

PRINCESS MONA

Palmist and Life Reader and "Little Snowball"

Ethics

If most of your career is spent reading in public, at parties, at corporate events, and at trade shows, you will hopefully have learned the value of keeping your readings short, fun, exciting, and entertaining. You may work with a disclaimer (such as, "for entertainment purposes only") that keeps your moral compass in sharp focus for you.

Likewise, if you read in a private office or by telephone, you will understand the value of having a compassionate approach to clients in need of counseling and support, who may come to you in a vulnerable state of mind, struggling with serious troubles, family tragedies, and financial crises. You may find yourself working without a disclaimer, by Spirit, perhaps as a minister, your moral compass also in sharp focus.

A third viewpoint is available as well: You may see the territory between party readings and private consultations as a continuum through which you can move at will, shifting the emphasis of your approach as you move from public entertainer to private counsellor, according to the day's agenda.

But whether you choose to stand on one side of a sharp moral dividing line or cheerfully traverse a continuum of approaches, what is actually important (and it is certainly more important than guessing at the moral motivations of the other readers whom you meet!) is to treat your clients with respect, decency, and fairness.

We all know what a fraudulent reader is, and I think we all agree that fraudulent reading is bad — bad for the client, bad for those of us who are counsellors, bad those of us who are party readers, and bad for the standing of the divinatory arts in society.

Words To Live By

As a reader, is it important to abide by a personal code of ethics? I think so.

Is it important to abide by a published or posted Code of Ethics? Again, I think so, although subscribing to a formal and explicit code is one of those very personal choices that we each must make for ourselves.

A Code of Ethics is a statement about who you are as a reader and what you provide to your clientele. It's as much an agreement between you and yourself as it is an agreement between you and society.

You can be a fantastic reader and beautifully serve your clients without ever having a published or posted Code of Ethics.

That being said, I'm a big fan of anything that helps focus purpose, for anyone.

If a Code of Ethics helps you define who you are, what you want to be, how you are going to do it, and what you stand for, then marvellous! Go right ahead!

My favourite Code of Ethics, and the one I live by, is the one published by the Association of Independent Readers and Root Workers (AIRR), a group of which I am a member. Along with a Code of Ethics, AIRR also has a Code of Conduct, which I particularly like, also.

I reprint them both here, with the kind permission of the Board of Bishops of Missionary Independent Spiritual Church, the group which governs the Association of Independent Readers and Rootworkers. Visit them online (and see me, too) at http://readersandrootworkers.org.

AIRR Code of Ethics

• I will become aware of the laws of the county, state, province, or nation in which I am practicing. I will strive to conform to those laws in my practice as a psychic reader and conjure worker.

• I will dedicate myself to providing compassionate and competent services. Within the scope of my knowledge, training, and experience, I will serve all my clients to the best of my abilities.

• I will represent myself to the public with a standard of professionalism. I will be honest and upright in my dealings with clients and colleagues, and I will encourage and assist others to maintain this standard.

• I will respect the personal rights of my clients, colleagues, and other professionals. I will safeguard the privacy of my clients and I will not slander, misrepresent, or make comparisons in a negative manner toward my competitors, colleagues, fellow workers in AIRR, or AIRR itself.

• I will continue to study, apply, and advance my knowledge and understanding of divination, hoodoo, conjure, rootwork, and related fields. I will ever strive to become more proficient in my practices in order to better serve my clients.

• When a client's requirements are outside my scope of spiritual practice or area of specialization, I will notify him or her of such. If possible, I will recommend one or more AIRR practitioners with qualifications in that area of spiritual practice or specialization.

• If I believe that a client may be in need of mental health evaluation or care, medical examination or treatment, or legal advice or services, and I am not personally qualified in such fields, I will refer her or him to a qualified professional or agency. If necessary I will postpone my services until I am assured that he or she is receiving competent mental health, medical, or legal services.

• I will not misrepresent myself or my services while advertising. I will not make promises, guarantees, or claims of results that are false in order to increase interest in my advertisements.

• I will not attempt to conceal my contact methods from the public. In addition to a contact name, my advertising materials will contain at least one of the following valid contact methods: telephone number, email address, street address.

• I will not engage in identity theft, plagiarism, or copyright violations. I will not substitute the photograph or image of another person to represent myself, nor will I publish photographs or texts describing the spiritual works of another person to represent them as my own.

AIRR Code of Conduct

• Ethical Psychic Readers and Hoodoo Rootworkers do not charge more than agreed upon with each client. There are no "hidden fees" or "add-ons" after a stated price is agreed upon for the psychic reading or the conjure work to be performed.

• Ethical Psychic Readers and Hoodoo Rootworkers expediently assist clients whose cases they accept. They set reasonable working hours and they do not "dodge" phone calls from clients that are received during those hours.

• Ethical Psychic Readers and Hoodoo Rootworkers do not claim that their spell-casting efforts will succeed "100%" or "in 24 hours" nor make any "guarantees." In the event that obstacles are encountered in their work, they inform their clients honestly and they set reasonable limitations on how long the work can be expected to proceed before the case is considered to be intractable.

• Ethical Psychic Readers and Hoodoo Rootworkers do not take financial or social advantage of clients with perceived psychological, medical, or legal problems. Whenever possible, they suggest appropriate and practical medical, legal, and social services to their clients that are supportive of the reading and the rootwork. They do not attempt to convince a client to renounce or refuse appropriate medical, legal, or social services.

• Ethical Psychic Readers and Hoodoo Rootworkers do not engage in any activities harmful to their clients. They do not engage in financial fraud, psychological abuse or domination, sexual seduction or molestation, personal deception, or unscrupulous magical manipulations of their clients.

• Ethical Psychic Readers and Hoodoo Rootworkers do not provide advice of a legal, financial, or medical nature. They do not supply advice which is significantly beyond their areas of actual training and competence, or for which they are not legally licensed or accredited.

• Ethical Psychic Readers and Hoodoo Rootworkers do not harass or abuse clients or other rootworkers. No matter what differences of opinion arise, they do not engage in disrespectful, aggressive, mean-spirited, unwantedly sexual, revengeful, or malevolent behaviour.

• Ethical Psychic Readers and Hoodoo Rootworkers do not require that their clients be exposed to dangerous chemicals or hazardous situations. While engaged in conjure services, they do not expose clients to hazards such as liquid Mercury, nor do they urge clients to expose themselves to peril in the procurement of unusual magical objects and substances.

• Ethical Psychic Readers and Hoodoo Rootworkers do not traffic in rare and endangered species of animals or plants. They refuse client requests to procure materials on the CITES list, or items that are illegal to collect or possess. They do not engage in animal cruelty or animal torture, as defined by the laws of their regions, states, or nations. They refuse client requests to engage in animal cruelty or animal torture.

The Beginning

So, there you have it, the book I've been waiting twenty years for someone to write.
I must say that I am jealous.
You now have a true "Heads Up" about the major professional arenas of our business.
The easiest thing now would be to drop this book in a dusty corner and tell yourself that someday you will implement the ideas presented here.

I sincerely hope you don't do that.

Everyone worries so much about silly things like competition, being "good enough," dealing with a variable income, and dealing with rejection.
These fears can stop you from taking the next few steps and creating your successful psychic career.
The truth about all of these fears is this:

Competition: There is no such thing as competition in our field. We are all so unique that there is no comparison. There are far more clients than we readers can ever handle. You have no competition.

"Good Enough": What in the heck does this mean, anyway? Perfect? There are no perfect readers! Decide what clientele you wish to serve, and what you can do for them. Learn to do this well (and define that; decide what it means). Do your best, stay in your integrity. That will be more than Good Enough, I promise.

The Variable Income Thing: A "real job" with a salary is actually a much more vulnerable situation. A professional reader cannot be fired. If you want more clients, do more marketing. You are completely in control of your success and your cash flow. Have some discipline and a plan.

Rejection: Not everyone is going to love you or say yes to your ideas. If you are an adult, this really cannot be a surprise to you! Just love what you are doing and keep pitching those ideas; with enough of them, some will stick and be productive. That is how it works. Don't take it personally.

So, there you go.
It's now time for you to get serious and design your future!
I look forward to hearing about your success!

Sincerely,
Valentina Burton

Valentina reading for a client in her office

The mysterious David Alexandre in his office

Reading at Hotel Zaza

Valentina reading cards at a trade show

A circus-themed baby shower

Val Moroccan

Mardi Gras

Entertainment for a Bollywood-themed wedding reception

Being creative with party fortune telling
Valentina as Lucy Van Pelt

Even if the party or event has no real theme,
always look special and interesting:
Valentina at Student Union Party at Texas Christian University

The Snow Queen reads cards at a Christmas party.